For

Stay heassant!

AP

A.P. Harrison

9. 8. 14

# Incessant Theology

## Alan P Harrison

Copyright © 2014 by Alan P Harrison

The right of Alan P Harrison to be identified as the author of this work has been asserted by him in accordance with the Copyright, Designs and Patents Act 1988.

All rights reserved. No part of this publication may be reproduced or transmitted in any form or by any means, electronic or mechanical, including photocopy, recording or any information storage and retrieval system, without permission in writing from the author.

First published in the UK in 2014.

ISBN 978-1-291-91723-9

Unless otherwise stated, Scripture quotations are from The Holy Bible, English Standard Version® (ESV®), copyright © 2001 by Crossway, a publishing ministry of Good News Publishers. Used by permission. All rights reserved.

Every effort has been made to trace copyright holders and to obtain their permission for the use of copyright material. The author apologizes for any errors or omissions in the above list and would be grateful if notified of any corrections that should be incorporated in future reprints or editions of this book.

www.IncessantTheology.com

# Acknowledgements

## ✳✳✳

This book could not have happened without the following people;

Sarah, for believing in me, for being my best friend, proof-reader and inspiration.

Desmond, for teaching me more about the love of God than a decade of studying the Bible.

Stanley, Pauline and Jo, for all the years of love, prayer and investment, and for being a safe place to be myself.

Andy, Sue and Tim, for treating me as one of your own.

Hope Church Glasgow, for affirming who God has made me to be, and spurring me on into ever greater things.

Partick Thursday Small Group, for being yourselves.

Sharpes, McAdam and Spybey, for unmitigated friendship.

The Bay Church, for solid foundations.

International Christian College, for training me in being a rightful handler of the word of truth.

Hermitage Academy and Dumbarton Academy, for years of employment in wonderful workplaces.

Andy Merrick and Daniel Johnson, for being the voices in my head.

Simon Parnham, for being my theological sounding board.

This book is dedicated to Rev. Arthur H. Howell,
for running the race well,
for being faithfully steadfast,
and for a lifetime of loving Jesus.

"On the mount of crucifixion,
Fountains opened deep and wide,
Through the floodgates of God's mercy,
Flowed a vast and gracious tide.


Grace and love like mighty rivers,
Poured incessant from above,
And Heaven's peace and perfect justice,
Kissed a guilty world in love"


'Here is Love'

William Rees, 1900

# Contents

# One

# Introduction

### ✳✳✳

The purpose of this book is to unite two distinct areas of Christianity; measured, exegetical theology and the identity, activity and presence of the Holy Spirit. Too often these two areas are at odds with one another, each claiming that the other is too far removed from being a legitimate expression of Christian faith and practise. While there is certainly no lack of theological works, or indeed writings concerning the Holy Spirit, it is rare, in my experience, for these two spheres to be found within the same book. Theologians often distrust experience; those with experience often distrust theologians.

I don't believe that these two areas need be, nor indeed should be, separate disciplines. Rather, I believe that for each of these aspects to be independent of the other leads to heresy or, at 'best', a disjointed Christianity. In this book, I wish to show those who believe in the power of the Bible, as well as those who believe in the power of the Holy Spirit, that it is possible to be both faithful to Scripture as well as being continually renewed by the Spirit.

While writing my dissertation for my honours degree in 2008 and 2009, I sought to understand the link, if there was one, between the work of the Holy Spirit in a church and the number of people who were saved in that church (see appendix, page 203). However, I was surprised by the lack of literature concerning the Holy Spirit in Christian book shops. Of course, the Holy Spirit was referred to innumerable times in systematic theology works, Trinitarian theology books and in statements of faith. But there seems to be a dearth of theological works specifically about the person of the Holy Spirit in Scripture.

This might be because there is a significant proportion of the church which holds to a cessationist viewpoint. If you don't believe that the Holy Spirit still brings the gifts today that He brought to the first apostles, then why spend time and energy thinking and studying Him? I held this viewpoint for several years, but I found that the more I looked at what the Bible said about the Holy Spirit, the more difficult it became to legitimately hold a cessationist position. This is explained in more depth in chapter 2.

In recent years, as the position of the cessationist has enjoyed a shrinking sphere of influence, more and more churches have revised their mission statements to include the person and work of the Holy Spirit as more than just a footnote. However, their practise doesn't seem to reflect this edit, and their meetings, preaching, worship and community remains practically cessationist, while being nominally continuationist. It is my belief that the majority of British churches sit in this category, though there may be a variety of reasons as to why this is.

The first reason could be simple tradition. While protestants, and evangelicals in particular, are rightly sceptical of tradition, I wonder how much we actually allow it to creep into our churches. As Californian pastor Rick Warren writes, the favourite phrase of tradition-driven churches is 'we've always done it this way', and the goal of these churches is to perpetuate the past[1].

If church leaders have never seen or experienced the manifest presence and power of the Holy Spirit, or been astonished by His gifts, then their church may be built on the assumption that their experience is the correct and commonly held one. This is fair enough, because nobody believes that they are wrong. If they did believe they were wrong, they would change their beliefs to ones

---

[1] R. Warren, *'The Purpose Driven Church'*, Michigan: Zondervan, 1995, p77

they deemed to be 'right'. But because nobody thinks they're wrong, that inversely can mean that everyone thinks they're right.

The second reason for on-going practical cessationism often compounds the first, that being negative or exaggerated experiences of the Holy Spirit which have been seen in other people or churches. If a person or a church does not expect the Holy Spirit to be miraculously present in any given meeting, but then find themselves in a situation where the Holy Spirit *is* present, or at least is claimed to be present, this can be unusual and even uncomfortable. I believe this is partly because people like to feel in control, and when there are manifestations of supernatural activity, even Biblical ones, we can feel out of control and therefore become uneasy. Alternatively, fear may emerge due to people being afraid of that which is different from them. They have perhaps heard stories or met people who claim to have had astonishing encounters, such as casting out demons, raising the dead, seeing amputated legs re-grow, having heavenly experiences or else simply being comfortable with using the phrase 'Jesus said this to me'. If your church culture has no category for these kinds of things, then either one needs to revise the categories, which can be painful, or else dismiss these claims (or 'this' person or 'that' church) as being unbiblical, which can be divisive.

I don't mean for this to sound aggressive, because I know of many churches that would fit the category of 'cessationist' (either nominally or doctrinally) and yet love Jesus passionately. Also, I believe that being hesitant to embrace unknown elements of Christianity often comes from a pastoral heart to keep the flock safe. This is a good, Godly attribute. However, if we forbid or prevent divine supernatural activity on the rationale that 'people might get hurt or upset', we run the risk of stifling, quenching and grieving the Holy Spirit[2], which is strictly written against in Scripture. We become like Marlin in 'Finding Nemo', who laments at the disappearance of

---

[2] Ephesians 4:30, 1 Thessalonians 5:19

his son saying that he'd promised to never let anything happen to him. His simple friend Dori replies that this was an odd sentiment, because that would mean that *nothing* would ever happen to him[3]. To grow in life, love and faith, people must be able to fail, get it wrong or be hurt. "The righteous man falls seven times and rises again"[4]. If we're righteous in Christ, we can fall, get it wrong or get hurt, and we'll rise again.

But more than this, a cessationist position presents a Christianity which is inherently contradictory; to claim that God is trinity, three divine persons in one God, but that one of these persons is effectively in semi-retirement compared to His former activities seems silly. Also, believing that (or acting like) the Holy Spirit has ceased operating in the manner which He did in Scripture presents us with the huge problem of pursuing Biblical models. If Jesus walked in the power of the Spirit, but the Spirit does not empower in the same way anymore, how can we emulate Jesus? Similarly, if David or Moses or Abraham or Peter or Paul or Timothy knew the manifest presence of the Spirit which we cannot know, are we left with an impotent Christianity, a pattern we are unable to follow? We might get to go to heaven (if indeed the Spirit can still apply the atoning sacrifice of Christ to our lives), but we certainly can't fulfil the great commission.

On the other side of the coin is the Christian who believes that the Holy Spirit is alive and well, who has regular conversations with God, who sees things that aren't physically there and who sees every situation through a spiritual lens. This type of Christian tends to flock to hear every travelling speaker with the title of 'prophet', 'healer' or 'presence bringer'. They are very sincere, very passionate about God and very disliking of any assertion that their experiences may be 'emotionalism', that they have an 'over-realised eschatology' or that

---

[3] 'Finding Nemo', 2003. Film. Directed by Andrew Stanton. USA: Buena Vista Pictures
[4] Proverbs 24:16

'they're just seeking attention'. Though it might not be said or even thought, these Christians can pay less attention to study of the Bible, subconsciously asking 'why would I need to read the book that God wrote when I can speak to the author Himself?'

The problem with this point of view is that it rejects Jesus as the model for Christianity. Jesus was found aged 12 in the temple with the scribes and scholars, asking questions and learning, as well as amazing them with His insights. Jesus quoted Deuteronomy three times to rebuke Satan while he was being tempted in the wilderness. Jesus said outrageous things like "it is easier for heaven and earth to pass away than for one dot of the Law to become void"[5]. A continuationist Christian is accused of not taking the Bible seriously, of overlooking key biblical passages in order to justify their practise and of prizing experience over service.

Indeed, it is true that some people who have claimed to have charismatic gifts have, in the end, turned out to be morally bankrupt or else be defrauding or scamming people. It is also true that because these types of people exist, who prey on those in real need of a touch from God or who need a miracle, that the reputation of Charismatic and Pentecostal Christians has been negatively affected. They are the very definition of 'those who take the name of the LORD in vain', of whom the LORD says 'they will not be held guiltless'[6]. Of course, all sins are forgivable in Christ, but manipulating or tricking people is not something which operates out of the Spirit of Christ.

That being said, having a poor experience of something should not preclude us from seeking a pure, authentic experience of something. If someone has abused the ministry of the Spirit for their own ends, this does not mean that everyone who has such a ministry is similarly corrupt. Does hearing a poor sermon mean all sermons are poor? Of course not, and neither does it mean that abusive use of

---

[5] Luke 16:17
[6] Exodus 20:7

the Holy Spirit should prevent us seeking the correct ministry of the Holy Spirit.

This book is a plea to both types of Christian; a plea to charismatics to be more reformed, and a plea to reformed Christians to be more charismatic. I do not believe that the best expression of true Christianity is to isolate the Holy Spirit from the Bible, nor to say or believe that a person must choose to be *either* biblically faithful *or* full of the Spirit. I believe, as I will demonstrate over the coming chapters, that to be faithful to Scripture is to be a charismatic Christian, and to be a charismatic Christian is to be faithful to Scripture.

# Two

# What is 'Incessant Theology'?

**\*\*\***

Before we launch into a lengthy discussion about incessant theology, it would be useful to clarify some of our terms. In this chapter I will explain what I mean by 'theology', as well as why theology can be 'incessant'. At the end of the book there is a glossary which contains brief explanations of some of the other terms used throughout this book, but the idea behind the book rests on two main premises; firstly that we can, in fact, know things about God and secondly that the Holy Spirit continues to bless the church with all the gifts He did in Scripture. If either of these two premises proves to be untrue or unjustified, then this book has little to say.

So as to be clear what I mean when I use the term 'theology', I will clarify it here. You will not find the word 'theology' in the Bible, nor will you find the word 'Bible' or 'trinity'. These are words which we, the church, have appropriated in order to explain or describe various ideas. 'Theology', broadly speaking, is talking about God. It is the study of God, and the study of God through his Word. We can know things about God because He has revealed these things to us. When I use the word 'theology', I am meaning 'things we know about God'. We can look to the Bible for insight about God, because "All Scripture is breathed out by God and [is] profitable for teaching"[7]. The Bible is particularly useful with reference to things of the Holy Spirit, as just seeing a miraculous sign does not always lead people to the right conclusion. When Paul was gathering sticks after being shipwrecked, a snake leapt from the wood and bit him on his hand. The native people he was with believed that this was divine retribution and,

---

[7] 2 Timothy 3:16

assuming Paul was therefore a murderer, waited around for him to drop dead. When this didn't happen, the native people changed their minds and said that, since he had been spared from the sea and from the snake, he was a god[8]. Their assumption was incorrect on both occasions; they saw a miracle, but got the explanation wrong. We need teaching and theology to explain the miraculous.

The idea for this book came during a small group meeting. One week during a time of worship, a friend of mine led us in a particularly outstanding rendition of William Rees' 'Here is Love, Vast as the Ocean', and one line in particular resonated in my mind more than any other;

> "Grace and Love, like mighty rivers, poured incessant from above, And Heav'ns peace and perfect justice kissed a guilty world in love."

While I am always quick to point out that an inspiring song does not have the same authority as inspired Scripture, I found myself pondering this line long after the song, and the meeting, had finished. Was the grace and love poured out like a mighty river truly incessant; truly done without ceasing? It was curious that the word 'incessant' has the same root as the phrase used to describe Christians who believe that the gifts of the Holy Spirit now are no longer available to the church; 'cessationist'. This line gave me the idea for 'Incessant Theology'; a theology of the continuing work of the Holy Spirit in the life, work and mission of the Church.

The purpose of this chapter is to outline why I believe it is entirely Biblical to believe that the gifts and activity of the Spirit are not only available, but are necessary for building a healthy church which fulfils the great commission. The cessationist argument states that Jesus, the 70 (or 72) and the apostles, including Paul, were able to perform miracles, but that with the death of the last of the apostles in approximately 100 A.D., these gifts ceased being available. The

---

[8] Acts 28:3-6

reason given for this is that the gifts of the Holy Spirit were poured out at Pentecost in order to 'jump start' the church into life and into activity, as the only point of reference that the early church had for its faith and practise was Jesus, who had returned to Heaven. These gifts continued until the New Testament was written, and since the Bible is God-breathed, it now functions *in place of* the miraculous work of the Holy Spirit.

While this viewpoint seems perfectly plausible, it ironically lacks much Biblical basis. The argument that the gifts have ceased is usually based around four passages of Scripture, these being 1 Corinthians 13:8-12, 2 Corinthians 12:12, Hebrews 1:1-2 and Hebrews 2:3-4. We will briefly look at these passages in order to understand what they are saying, as well as taking a brief survey of the New Testament.

**1 Corinthians 13:8-12**

> "Love never ends. As for prophecies, they will pass away; as for tongues, they will cease; as for knowledge, it will pass away. For we know in part and we prophesy in part, but when the perfect comes, the partial will pass away. When I was a child, I spoke like a child, I thought like a child, I reasoned like a child. When I became a man, I gave up childish ways. For now we see in a mirror dimly, but then face to face. Now I know in part; then I shall know fully, even as I have been fully known."[9]

This verse is very clear; prophesies will pass away, tongues will pass away and knowledge will pass away. Given the context of 'prophesies' and 'tongues', we can appropriately assume that the 'knowledge' being spoken of here is a 'word of knowledge', as opposed to the general ability to know something. It would be very strange for Paul to mention prophesy, tongues and knowledge in

---

[9] 1 Corinthians 13:8-12

both the preceding[10] and following[11] chapters, but to have a different meaning of 'knowledge' in chapter 13 alone. But one thing is clear; these gifts will cease. The obvious question for us to ask, then, is 'when did/will these gifts cease?' The passage refers to a time when we prophesy in part, presumably the present day for Paul, but that when the 'perfect' comes, the partial (tongues, prophesy and knowledge, etc.) will pass away. Paul then makes a comparison to the use of prophesy, tongues and knowledge with being a child, and to giving up these 'childish ways' upon reaching adulthood.

Up until this point, we have no idea of the identity of this 'perfect' Paul is referring to. However, verse 12 gives us a big clue. "Now we see in a mirror dimly, but then face to face. Now I know in part; then I shall know fully, even as I have been fully known." The time at which the gifts will cease is explained as being the time when the 'perfect' will appear. The 'perfect', according to verse 12, will have a face, just as I have a face, and will fully know the one whom He is looking at. The identity of the instigator of the end of the gifts is a person, as they have a face, is a person who can be described as 'perfect', and is a person who knows and is known. The context of chapter 13 gives an explanation of the threads of thought in chapter 12, that being building up the body of Christ. There seems to be little doubt that the person in question in chapter 13 is Jesus Christ.

The assertion that the 'perfect' in chapter 13 is actually the final and completed canon of Scripture, which was closed to being edited upon the death of the last of the twelve apostles, has no basis in Scripture. Ironically, in an attempt to preserve a high-view of Scripture, some have read their own interpretations and experiences *into* the Bible, a dangerous process called eisegesis. There is no reference to a book, or to God's word, or to Scripture anywhere in this chapter, or even in the first 14 chapters of 1 Corinthians. Rather, the absence of even a shred of evidence that 'perfect' in this passage

---

[10] 1 Corinthians 12:8-10
[11] 1 Corinthians 14:6

refs to the Bible and the strong assertion that it refers to Christ, points to the gifts ceasing at Christ's second coming, and not at the finishing of the Bible. Since the second coming will be a global and public event[12], and it hasn't yet happened, we can safely conclude that this passage is declaring that the gifts *will* cease, but they haven't ceased yet.

**2 Corinthians 12:12**

Our next passage to consider is also a letter of Paul to the church in Corinth;

> "The signs of a true apostle were performed among you with utmost patience, with signs and wonders and mighty works."[13]

Some Jesus-loving Christians (because you can be charismatic, cessationist, Roman Catholic, Orthodox, Reformed or Episcopalian and still love Jesus) have claimed that the above verse is proof that the gifts have ceased; assuming that 'signs and wonders' are synonymous with 'gifts of the Spirit'. These cessationists believe that only the twelve disciples and Paul were 'true apostles', and therefore none exist today. As such, their interpretation of this verse as saying that signs and wonders can only be performed by a true apostle leads them to the conclusion that signs and wonders have ceased.

However, the argument that only the twelve disciples were apostles, and so were the only ones to perform signs and wonders, doesn't hold much water, as the New Testament uses this term with reference to numerous individuals beyond the twelve. There seem to be various 'categories' of apostle. Jesus is referred to as an 'apostle and high priest of our confession[14]', and while few would argue that

---

[12] Revelation 1:7
[13] 2 Corinthians 12:12

modern apostles were in the same category as Him, fewer still would also argue that Jesus doesn't exist today on the basis that apostles don't exist. There are the twelve apostles, including Judas Iscariot, whom Jesus personally appointed[15], but there is also Matthias[16], who was appointed by the remaining 11 apostles after Judas hung himself. Most people would recognise Paul as an apostle[17], even though he didn't enjoy the same training with Jesus during His earthly ministry, and Barnabus is also named as an apostle in the same breath as Paul[18]. Additionally, Andronicus and Junia, who are listed as 'outstanding among' or 'of note among' the apostles[19], depending on your translation, indicating that these two were not only apostles, but were exceptional examples. Interestingly, Junia is widely regarded as being a feminine name, suggesting that being an apostle is not only not limited to the twelve disciples, but is a gift that any person, regardless of gender, can exhibit. And finally, Paul has no problem as listing Silvanus and Timothy as apostles alongside himself to the Thessalonian church[20].

As a final point regarding apostles, many cessationists assert that the main purpose of the apostles was to write Scripture, which replaced the need for signs and wonders and spiritual gifts. However, this belief also seems to be built on shaky ground. Of the twelve original apostles, only five of them wrote any Scripture, those being Matthew, John, James, Peter and Jude. Paul was certainly an apostle, though not one of the twelve, and he wrote much of the New Testament, but most notably, non-apostle Luke wrote, word-for-word, the largest percentage of the New Testament. So, to say that the purpose of an apostle is to write Scripture would mean that

---

[14] Hebrews 3:1
[15] Matthew 10:1-5
[16] Acts 1:26
[17] Romans 1:1, 1 Corinthians 1:1, Galatians 1:1, etc.
[18] Acts 14:14
[19] Romans 16:7
[20] 1 Thessalonians 2:6 (see 1 Thessalonians 1:1)

either we should discount seven of the disciples who didn't write any, or else include Luke as an apostle, quite without any Biblical hint that he was one.

The fact that the marks of a true apostle are signs and wonders does not give us a proof-text for the cessation of supernatural occurrences, but rather gives us criteria by which to measure those with the gift of being an apostle. Similarly, manifesting the gifts of the Spirit is not limited to those with the title of 'apostle', and there are many examples of people in Scripture who were not apostles but who still exhibited signs and wonders. Those in the upper room at Pentecost were not all apostles (less than 10% were) and they were *all* filled with the Holy Spirit and spoke in tongues[21]. Stephen was 'full of grace and power and was doing great wonders and signs among the people'[22], Philip was given a hearing by the crowds because they 'saw the signs that he did'[23], which included 'many who were paralysed or lame [being] healed'[24] and Ananias was instrumental in bringing the Gospel to the gentiles by having the faith to lay hands on Paul to regain his sight[25].

In the middle of Peter's sermon to Cornelius and those in his household, the Holy Spirit fell on those listening and they began speaking in tongues. This was amazing to the Jews who were also present as Cornelius and his household were gentile, and yet they received the same blessing as the Jewish believers at Pentecost, resulting in many getting saved[26]. Later in Acts, a previously unknown believer named Agabus, most certainly not an apostle, is mentioned twice as prophesying about a famine in the Roman world,[27] as well as warning Paul that he would be bound if he were to go

---

[21] Acts 2:4
[22] Acts 6:8
[23] Acts 8:6
[24] Acts 8:7
[25] Acts 9:17-18
[26] Acts 10:44-48
[27] Acts 11:28

down to Jerusalem[28]. On both occasions, Agabus is referred to as a prophet, and is recorded as speaking by or for the Holy Spirit. Acts 13 records that the church at Antioch has prophets, some of whom were apostles, such as Barnabus, yet some weren't[29].

In his ministry to the Ephesian church, Paul learns that while the believers there had been baptised into John's baptism of repentance, they had not received the Holy Spirit, and so Paul baptised them 'in the name of the Lord Jesus', and they spoke in tongues and prophesied[30]. Paul's letter to the Galatian churches mentions that they were seeing miracles being worked among them by the Spirit[31], and his famous first letter to the Corinthian church was, if anything, a plea to maximise the effect of spiritual gifts rather than having them abused or lost in a flurry of over-excitement[32]. These gifts were being used by the church, not limited to an apostle. Paul also writes to the Thessalonians not to despise prophesy or quench the Spirit, presumably because some people in the church were prophesying and others were despising it[33], and also to Timothy not to forget the prophesies given about him when the leaders laid hands on him and prayed[34].

The purpose of outlining this rather exhaustive list of people other than apostles who were blessed with spiritual gifts is to demonstrate that the Spirit's blessing to the church was not of limited scope. It was not restricted to only a few, now dead, individuals and is therefore still relevant to today's churches; the Spirit still brings gifts to the church, because the church still has work to do.

---

[28] Acts 21:10-11
[29] Acts 13:1
[30] Acts 19:1-7
[31] Galatians 1:5
[32] 1 Corinthians 14:1-40
[33] 1 Thessalonians 5:19-20
[34] 1 Timothy 1:18-19, 4:14

## Hebrews 1:1-2

> "Long ago, at many times and in many ways, God spoke to our fathers by the prophets, but in these last days he has spoken to us by his Son, whom he appointed the heir of all things, through whom also he created the world."[35]

The writer to the Hebrews, whomever that may be, opens the epistle with the above words. These verses can be interpreted as saying that, while God used to speak to His people by prophets ('in many ways'), now, in the last days, He has spoken to us through the coming of Jesus. The argument goes that, while the prophets were necessary in the Old Covenant, now Jesus has been incarnated, crucified, resurrected and has ascended, the need for prophesy has ended. There are, however, a few problems with using this passage as a justification for cessationism.

Firstly, as was the case with 2 Corinthians 12:12, in order to read the passage through cessationist eyes, you need to presuppose a cessationist viewpoint. This is firstly because Hebrews 1 does not mention Scripture at all. It does mention Christ "upholding the universe by the word of His power"[36], but this is referring to his power being given through a word, rather than His Word (i.e. Scripture) sustaining the universe. So, in order to make the passage fit a cessationist argument, you must read *into* the text something to the effect of 'in these last days He has spoken to us by his Son, whom we can read about in the Bible and by the Bible we can know Him'. While this sentiment is true up to a point, it negates the work of the Holy Spirit and, more importantly, isn't present in the text.

The second reason why this text should not be used to support a cessationist viewpoint is that the very time the writer had pen in hand to write this epistle, prophesy, tongues, miracles and signs and wonders were going on in churches all around the world. If the

---

[35] Hebrews 1:1-2
[36] Hebrews 1:3

mission of Jesus was meant to put an end to the gifts, then what are we to do with Pentecost? Remember, Pentecost happened *after* the earthly mission of Christ had come to a conclusion, but *before* this letter to the Hebrews was written. While it is true that we are in the last days, albeit being in between the beginning of the last days and actual last day, it would not be Biblically consistent to believe that the last days have concluded. It is true that the gifts will cease when we see Christ face to face[37], but until that time they will continue being needed and given in order for Jesus to build His church.

Finally, something which we must consider is the context in which each book of the Bible is written. The epistle to the Hebrews is, as the title suggests, a letter to Hebrew people, presumably who are trying to understand the new covenant of Christ in light of the old covenant of Moses. A friend of mine once described the book of Hebrews as 'The Old Testament for beginners', in that it is explaining Old Testament ideas, in Greek, to a New Testament audience. Keeping this in mind, it seems that these opening words are to view Christ against the backdrop of the Old Testament, and as being superior to the Old Testament prophets, who would speak the very words of God, whereas Christ is the Word of God incarnate. This idea marks a sizable shift in thinking, from looking to men who speak God's words as a pointer towards salvation, to looking to a man who *is* the Word of God and the *bringer* of salvation. And so it seems that Hebrews 1:1-2 is not speaking about the gift of prophesy ceasing, as this cannot be the case for reasons of chronology, but rather is speaking about the superiority of Christ over the Old Testament prophets, which few Christians would question.

### Hebrews 2:3-4

> "How shall we escape if we neglect such a great salvation? It was declared at first by the Lord, and it was attested to us by those who heard, while God also bore witness by

---

[37] 1 Corinthians 13:8-12

25

signs and wonders and various miracles and by gifts of the Holy Spirit distributed according to his will."[38]

In a similar way to 2 Corinthians 12, if you believe that the apostles were the only ones who could demonstrate spiritual gifts, then this passage seems to imply that signs and wonders and miracles and gifts of the Holy Spirit were available only to the apostles, i.e., 'those who heard'. Again, in order to read this passage in this way, you must assume certain things about the gifts of the Spirit and about apostles prior to reading it. This is not a helpful, nor indeed a biblically legitimate, way of approaching the text.

Furthermore, one must read this passage carefully in order to properly understand the message contained within. There is a clear distinction between two separate topics in question here. Firstly, the 'great salvation' which was first declared by the Lord and then attested to by 'those who heard', and secondly concerning the witness borne by signs, wonders, miracles and gifts of the Holy Spirit.

Notice that the 'it' in verse 3 is referring to the 'great salvation'. This means that it is the great salvation that was first declared by the Lord, and was attested to the writer by 'those who heard' (presumably the twelve, among others). But then, as if the message of Jesus and the testimony of the apostles wasn't enough, God 'also bore witness by signs and wonders...' etc. This demonstrates the difference and the similarity between the message of salvation and the witnessing of miraculous occurrences; the Gospel message should be proclaimed *and* demonstrated. It would be wrong to read this passage as saying that because the gifts of the Spirit were attested to by 'those who heard', and as these were presumably the apostles, that these gifts are now redundant. This would be to do origami with the passage, rather than letting the words say what they say.

---

[38] Hebrews 2:3-4

Finally, notice that the miracles, signs and wonders and gifts of the Holy Spirit were distributed 'according to His will'. The Holy Spirit is the Spirit of the living God, and indeed is fully God as much as Jesus and the Father are each fully God. This is not a book about the trinity, but it is important for us not to relegate the Holy Spirit to the 'third deity among many'. Where the Spirit is, the fullness of God is. We will deal more fully with the deity of the Holy Spirit in chapter 9, but for now it will suffice to say that the blessings that the Holy Spirit bestows are distributed according to the will of God as a witness to the great salvation secured for us by Jesus.

Therefore, in light of the apparent lack of biblical backing for the cessationist position, let us survey the Bible to establish the roles, works and person of the Holy Spirit, believing and assuming that He is the same today as He is in Scripture, and can impact the lives of believers today in the same way He did for the early church in the first century.

# Three

# The Spirit is a Gift and Brings Gifts

## ✳✳✳

And so we come to our Biblical survey. Over the next ten chapters we will look at the entirety of the role, work and person of the Holy Spirit in the Bible. This will give us a comprehensive understanding of who the Holy Spirit is and what He does. There are approximately 300 references to the Holy Spirit in the Bible, breaking down almost exactly into one quarter being in the Old Testament, and the remaining three quarters being in the New Testament. Some of the verses we will look at will describe more than one work or attribute of the Spirit, for example, the Spirit could be anointing someone, but that same person could also be prophesying, which is bringing a gift, and so is something separate.

One of the facets of the Holy Spirit which is debated between conservative, reformed Christians and charismatic Christians is the question of the gifts of the Spirit. The Bible is quite clear that the Holy Spirit is present, as we have seen, and the Bible is also pretty clear about what His presence looks like, as we shall see. The question we have to answer is; do we include the gifts of the Holy Spirit in our theology and practice as a compulsory footnote, or do we include the gifts of the Holy Spirit in our theology and practise as a wonderful blessing?

### The Spirit brings gifts in the Old Testament

The first occurrence in the Bible of the Spirit being specifically mentioned as giving a particular gift is to a man named Bezalel in Exodus 31. The LORD explains to Moses that He has called Bezalel by name and has filled him with the Spirit and with ability and intelligence to work artistically with precious metals[39], and with the skill of "any sort of workman or skilled designer"[40]. This is in the context of the construction of the tabernacle, and so his gifting was to bring worship to God.

Many years after Moses led the Israelites out of Egypt, he is presiding over a couple of million people and it becomes apparent that this is too much for one man to do alone. So, elders are appointed to help Moses, and the LORD "takes some of the Spirit that is on Moses and puts it onto the seventy elders", and they all prophesied[41]. However, two of those appointed as elders did not make it to the meeting with the LORD, and instead remained in the camp, but the Spirit rested on them nonetheless, and they began prophesying where they were. Upon hearing this Joshua, Moses' deputy, implores Moses to make them stop prophesying, presumably because he doesn't believe they are really prophesying as they hadn't been at the meeting. But Moses responds that he wishes that all people of the LORD were prophets, so that they would have the Spirit of the LORD put on them[42]. It seems that Moses knew thousands of years before Paul wrote to the Thessalonian church not to treat prophesy with contempt[43].

In the time of the Judges, the people of Israel were being oppressed by the king of Mesopotamia, and so God raised up a deliverer named Othniel. He was gifted with integrity and wisdom, and so judged Israel in an upright manner, because "the Spirit of the LORD was upon him"[44]. The people triumphed over their oppressors, and under his leadership the land had rest for forty years. Godly leadership prospers the people.

---

[39] Exodus 31:1-5
[40] Exodus 35:31-25
[41] Numbers 11:24-25
[42] Numbers 11:26-29
[43] 1 Thessalonians 5:20
[44] Judges 3:10

The story of Samson gives us a helpful insight into the ministry of the Spirit in bringing gifts. As Samson was going to see the woman whom he wanted to marry, a lion comes towards him roaring. What happens next is brilliantly described;

> "Then the Spirit of the LORD rushed upon him, and although he had nothing in his hand, he tore the lion in pieces."[45]

Samson's remarkable strength was the result of the Holy Spirit 'rushing upon him'. This is mentioned twice more in his story; once when he foolishly invents a riddle about the lion for his wife's people, the Philistines, and in his anger, when they trick an answer out of his wife, he struck down thirty of them. Also, when he had agreed to being handed over to the Philistines for the unwise crime of tying torches to foxes tails and using them to set barns on fire, the Spirit of the LORD rushes upon him, and he is able to break the ropes of his captors and slay a thousand Philistines. By all accounts, Samson was a hot-head, a man whom God blessed with great ability and strength, but who failed to exercise appropriate restraint. In the present new-covenant era, if we are blessed with the gifts of the Spirit[46] so as to not limit the gifts by our shortcomings.

This interesting description of the Spirit of God 'rushing upon' people is not limited to Samson. Saul, the first king of Israel, is also described as having this experience. When Samuel anoints Saul as king in 1 Samuel 10, Samuel gives some very specific and astonishing prophecies about what will happen to Saul, one being that the Spirit will 'rush upon him' when he meets with some worshipping prophets in Gibeath-elohim, and that Saul himself will also prophesy[47]. The result of this will be that he will 'be turned into another man', which means that God will give him a new heart[48]. All

---

[45] Judges 14:6
[46] Galatians 5:22-23
[47] 1 Samuel 10:6

of these things happen to Saul exactly as Samuel predicted[49]. Later, when Saul hears the news that Israel is being besieged by Jabesh-Gilead, he is greatly angered and, after the Spirit had 'rushed upon' him, took action to stir the men of Israel into defending their nation.[50]

However, as is well known, Saul did not remain a virtuous man all his life. He was consumed with jealousy concerning David, who would succeed him as king, and so we read in 1 Samuel 19 that he is seeking David in order to kill him. This chapter tells us that when the messengers of Saul find David with Samuel and other prophets prophesying, the messengers cannot help but prophesy themselves, because "the Spirit of God came on them"[51]. In response, Saul sends two more groups of messengers to see what's happening, and all of those messengers begin prophesying as well. Finally, Saul goes himself and also begins prophesying, because 'the Spirit of the LORD came upon him'[52]. The result of this was that people wondered whether Saul was also one of the Prophets[53]. When the Spirit is present and active, even the deepest hatred can be overcome.

The Holy Spirit inspired the gift of prophesy elsewhere in the Old Testament, such as giving the prophetic gift to Azariah in order to speak to King Asa[54], to Jahaziel in order for him to speak to the assembly of Judah[55] which caused them to worship with a very loud voice, and finally by 'clothing' Zechariah, who rebuked king Joash and the people of Judah for breaking the commandments of God, which resulted in his being killed by the people[56]. Nehemiah confirms that these Old Testament prophets were speaking by the Spirit[57],

---

[48] 1 Samuel 10:9
[49] 1 Samuel 10:10
[50] 1 Samuel 11:6
[51] 1 Samuel 19:20
[52] 1 Samuel 19:23
[53] 1 Samuel 19:24
[54] 2 Chronicles 15:1-8
[55] 2 Chronicles 20:13-19
[56] 2 Chronicles 24:20-22

and Ezekiel's experience of the Spirit of the LORD 'falling on him' and telling him what to say gives weight to this[58].

However, it is the book of Joel that causes us to pause and consider the Old Testament perspective on the role of the Spirit bringing gifts in the New Testament era. The famous prophesy (itself inspired by the Spirit) given by Joel explains that in the last days the ministry of the Spirit to bring gifts will not be limited to a small demographic of people. Joel asserts that God will pour out his Spirit on all flesh; sons and daughters, old and young, servants and free people will be blessed by the Spirit of God[59]. It will no longer be just those with the title of either 'prophet', 'priest' or 'king' who will be blessed with the gifts of prophesy, dreams and visions, among others. Rather, all flesh will be offered the gifts of the Spirit, because all flesh will be offered the salvation of the messiah. When Joel is writing, this is very much in the future, but with the gift of hindsight and the faithful record of Scripture, we can see the fulfilment of Joel's prophesy on the day of Pentecost[60], which was very much the beginning of the new covenant church which continues to this day.

**The Spirit brings gifts in the New Testament**

The first mention of the Holy Spirit bringing gifts in the New Testament era is made by Jesus, as He sends out the twelve disciples to heal the sick, raise the dead, cleanse lepers and cast out demons[61]. Jesus explains that this activity will result in them being hauled before kings and governors to explain themselves, but that they should not worry about what they will say, as in that hour the 'Spirit of the Father' will tell them what to say[62].

---

[57] Nehemiah 9:30
[58] Ezekiel 11:5
[59] Joel 2:28-29
[60] Acts 2:1-21
[61] Matthew 10:8
[62] Matthew 10:20

Later, when Jesus is quizzed about the source of the power by which He casts out demons, the Pharisees assert that he is doing so by the power of the devil. However, Jesus refutes this by pointing out to them that a kingdom divided against itself will fall, explaining that it is by the Spirit of God that He is casting out demons, and as such the Kingdom of God has come upon them[63].

Other than Zechariah, the father of John the Baptist, being filled with the Holy Spirit and prophesying about his son[64], and the much-debated passage from the end of the Gospel of Mark where Jesus commissions the disciples to cast out demons, speak in tongues and pick up snakes[65], these few references are all the four gospels can contribute to the discussion about the gifts of the Spirit. The majority of the material about the gifts comes from Acts and the epistles, to which we will now turn.

The book of Acts alone gives us more than 20% of the Biblical references to the gifts of the Spirit or the Spirit being a gift. This makes sense, as it is not until the day of Pentecost, recorded in Acts, that the Spirit is poured out on all flesh as Joel prophesied; it seems logical that once all flesh have access to the gifts of the Spirit that instances of their happening would increase.

Acts 2 gives us some great insight into the gifts of the Holy Spirit. This passage by no means speaks exclusively about the gifts, but we will consider the other aspects of the Holy Spirit mentioned here in later chapters. One of the first things that strikes the reader of Acts 2 is that it begins by explaining that the church, then numbering 120 people, was "all together in one place"[66]. This is almost certainly a reference to the geographical location of the believers, as they were in the same room, but it also could refer to a sense of unity which they felt. The Pentecost event could have happened during a meal,

---

[63] Matthew 12:28
[64] Luke 1:67-80
[65] Mark 16:15-18
[66] Acts 2:1

during a time of prayer, during an administrative meeting to discuss how to survive in a world which wanted them dead; we don't know. But we do know that they were all together. Psalm 133 speaks about the LORD commanding a blessing where the people dwell in unity[67], and although he was elsewhere being the best Pharisee he could be, the same Spirit who inspired Paul to write that the church "is being built together into a dwelling place for God by the Spirit"[68] was present at Pentecost. The point I'm making is that division leads to the death of a church, whereas unity in the Spirit leads to life. The early church instinctively knew this.

After the house was shaken and tongues of fire had rested on each person, they were all filled with the Spirit and began "speaking in other tongues"[69]. Notice that none of the people who were present were excluded; they *all* were filled with the Spirit and began speaking in tongues. This was an inclusive event with no sense of division or segregation; all who were present were filled with the Spirit and demonstrated a gift of the Spirit, in this case tongues. The crowd who were gathered outside was comprised of a myriad of different races, nationalities and languages, but each heard in their own language the telling of the mighty works of God[70]. This is certainly a miraculous event, and, if you seek them, there are anecdotal stories of this kind of miracle happening in contemporary churches. However, this is not the only use of the gift of tongues, as is explained in 1 Corinthians, and which we will come to later.

The response of the gathered crowd is split; some are perplexed, but others just think it's funny and that they're drunk. In order to explain what is going on, Peter gets up and preaches to them. He explains that the phenomenon that the crowd are currently witnessing was foretold long before by the prophet Joel, and his rationale for why they are not drunk is that it's only nine in the morning. Peter points

---

[67] Psalm 133:1-3
[68] Ephesians 2:22
[69] Acts 2:4
[70] Acts 2:11

out that Joel prophesied about a demonstrable shift that would occur when God pours out His Spirit on all flesh, this being that people from all demographics of life will prophesy[71]. Notice how Peter, and the writer Luke, closely connect speaking in tongues with prophesying, and also how in Acts 2:32 the work of the Trinity is so closely intertwined:

> "This Jesus God raised up, and of that we all are witnesses. Being therefore exalted at the right hand of God, and having received from the Father the promise of the Holy Spirit, he has poured out this that you yourselves are seeing and hearing."[72]

Peter is explaining that Jesus has been raised, and is now sat at the right hand of God the Father, who has poured out the promised Holy Spirit, and that this is what the crowd is currently witnessing. Pentecost was a Trinitarian event.

Along the same Trinitarian lines, when Peter is a guest in the house of Cornelius preaching to a gentile household, he gives a wonderfully succinct summary of the ministry of Jesus and the role that the Holy Spirit had therein. He explains that "God anointed Jesus with the Holy Spirit and with power", which was the catalyst for Him to go about doing good and healing all who were oppressed by the devil[73]. Jesus' miraculous ministry was fuelled by the ministry of the Holy Spirit, given by God the Father. We will discuss the anointing of the Holy Spirit on Jesus, and on the church, in chapter 12. Similarly, when Paul is at Ephesus, he lays hands on the disciples there who had not heard about the Holy Spirit, and they began speaking in tongues and prophesying[74]. Interestingly, Acts 19 also records the extent of Paul's miraculous ministry, which included his handkerchiefs and aprons being used to heal the sick and cast out

---

[71] Acts 2:17-18
[72] Acts 2:32-33
[73] Acts 10:38
[74] Acts 19:6

demons[75]. This kind of statement causes havoc with a western conservative mind-set, even one which is open to the continuing work of the Holy Spirit. However, if the ministry of the Holy Spirit is truly incessant, why can this sort of miraculous happening not occur today?

A member of the Jerusalem church journeyed to Antioch and prophesied by the Spirit that there would be a widespread famine. As a result of this, the disciples in this church determined to send relief to the brothers in Judea[76]. This radical generosity was prompted by a prophesy given by the Spirit. Elsewhere in Acts, the Spirit prompts a visiting prophet to the church in Caesarea to takes Paul's belt and bind his own hands, symbolising how Paul would be treated by the Jewish rulers and the Gentiles[77]. In the first instance, it causes the church to take action. In the second instance, the prophesy causes the church to reaffirm their mission, even unto death. In both instances, the church is strengthened by prophesy.

Upon the conclusion of Acts, we can turn to the writings of Paul and John, as well the writer to the Hebrews, for more insight into the gifts of the Spirit. As with every Biblical book, the epistles were written to a particular group of people in order to address a particular set of issues. However, the epistles were inspired by the Spirit and are a record of the early church for the benefit of the contemporary church. Because of this, we can trust their instruction about issues such as the gifts of the Spirit.

The manifest presence of the Spirit of God was very apparent in Paul's ministry, as he describes towards the end of Romans, saying that he sought only to speak of Christ and His using himself to bring the gentiles to faith, by word, deed, signs and wonders and by the power of the Spirit[78]. The combination of these elements of the

---

[75] Acts 19:11-12
[76] Acts 11:27-29
[77] Acts 21:7-14
[78] Romans 15:18-19

Christian life enabled him to "[fulfil] the ministry of the Gospel of Christ"[79]. Terry Virgo, founder of NewFrontiers family of churches, sees no conflict between the preaching of sound doctrine and the doing of amazing miracles, pointing out that Paul both wrote Romans and raised the dead[80]. Paul writes to the Corinthian church that he sought not to persuade them as to the deity of Christ with 'the wisdom of men', but by demonstrating the power of the Spirit to them[81].

Paul also writes much about the gifts of the Spirit to the church in Corinth, and it is his first letter which provides us with many details about spiritual gifts. He begins chapter twelve by affirming that there are many gifts, but that they all come from the same Spirit[82]. This is very helpful to hear, as there can be a tendency among some to believe that the more dramatic gifts, such as prophesy or healing, are more spiritual or more valuable than other less dramatic gifts. Paul is refuting this sentiment in this verse; there are varieties of gifts, but they all come from the same Spirit. The gifts are given to *all,* and that for the mutual blessing of the church[83]. Because of this we can conclude two things. Firstly, that no Christian is excluded from receiving the gifts of the Spirit, and secondly, the use of the gifts should benefit the whole church and not promote or elevate one person, or one type of gifting, over another. The Spirit gives gifts of wisdom, words of knowledge, faith, healing, miracles, prophesy, discernment of spirits, tongues and interpretation of tongues[84]. Paul affirms again in verse 11 that each gift is given by "one and the same Spirit, who apportions to each one individually as He wills"[85]. The Spirit is God, which we will explore more in chapter 9, and He distributes to each believer the gifts as He sees fit.

---

[79] Romans 15:19
[80] T. Virgo, *'The Spirit-Filled Church'*, Oxford: Monarch Books, 2011, p47
[81] 1 Corinthians 2:4-5
[82] 1 Corinthians 12:4
[83] 1 Corinthians 12:7
[84] 1 Corinthians 12:8-10
[85] 1 Corinthians 12:11

Paul spends the rest of chapter 12, all of chapter 13 and most of chapter 14 discussing spiritual gifts. He explains that the context in which the gifts are to be used, and indeed the context in which they are useful, is one of love. "If I speak in tongues but do not love, I am just making noise"[86], he effectively says. In the church today the gifts can be divisive, but this should not be the case, because if they are used in love in order to build people up, this will heal divisions rather than create them. Instead of shying away from the spiritual gifts because they might cause division, Paul urges us to earnestly desire them, especially prophesy[87]. Speaking in tongues is not discouraged, quite the opposite[88], but the gift of prophesy is to be especially sought. This is because when someone speaks in tongues, he builds himself up[89] and speaks to God by uttering mysteries in the Spirit[90], but no one can understand him. When someone prophesies the whole church is built up[91]. Those who are eager for manifestations of the Spirit should strive for them in love, and should strive for manifestations which build up the church[92].

Paul is at pains to stress his approval of speaking in tongues, almost bragging that he speaks in tongues more than any of the Corinthian church[93], but is clear that he is more concerned with the building up of the church than with any particular gifting. To speak five words of prophesy is of more worth then speaking ten thousand words in tongues[94], if this results in the church being built up. However, Paul also has in mind the distinctions between gifts which are for the benefit of believers and gifts which are for benefit of unbelievers; tongues being the former, prophesy being the latter[95]. His argument

---

[86] 1 Corinthians 13:1
[87] 1 Corinthians 14:1
[88] 1 Corinthians 14:5
[89] 1 Corinthians 14:4
[90] 1 Corinthians 14:2
[91] 1 Corinthians 14:4
[92] 1 Corinthians 14:12
[93] 1 Corinthians 14:18
[94] 1 Corinthians 14:19

is that if someone who is not a Christian comes across a group of Christians all speaking in tongues, they will think that the Christians are crazy. However, if that same person comes across a group of Christians and a prophesy is given, "he is convicted by all, he is called to account by all, the secrets of his heart are disclosed, and so, falling on his face, he will worship God and declare that God is really among you"[96]. If we needed no other motivation to earnestly seek to prophesy, having people come to know Christ as a result of prophesy would be a good place to start.

Paul goes on to explain that when a church comes together, everyone has something to contribute, and because of this, gifts should be used for mutual building up. Paul spent much time in 1 Corinthians appealing to the church to use the gifts to build people up. He makes his case by explaining that when the church is gathered, everyone has something to bring; a hymn, a lesson, a revelation, a tongue or an interpretation[97]. But Paul is not advocating by this that churches should be free-for-alls, and requires that no more than three people should speak in tongues, and each with an interpretation; if there is no one to interpret, they are to remain silent[98]. Similarly, only two or three prophets are to speak, and the others are to weigh what is said[99]. This is one of the main differences between Old Testament and New Testament prophesy. In the Old Testament, those who prophesied were few and far between, and they spoke the very words of God, frequently using the phrase 'thus says the LORD'. In the New Testament, those who prophesy are frequent, because the Spirit is poured out on *all* flesh, and the church is required to weigh what is said, rather than accepting every word a prophet says without question. If a prophesy given in a church today is contrary to the teaching of the Bible, it

---

[95] 1 Corinthians 14:23-25
[96] 1 Corinthians 14:24-25
[97] 1 Corinthians 14:26
[98] 1 Corinthians 14:27-28
[99] 1 Corinthians 14:29

should not be taken to heart, and the person bringing the prophesy should be lovingly given Biblical direction. Prophecies should be given one by one, so that people may learn and benefit from what is being shared, but all must be done in an orderly fashion, because God is a God of peace, not confusion[100]. Although Paul and Peter didn't always agree on everything, Peter's sentiments about the issue of prophesy are in line with Paul's. Peter writes that prophesy is given not by the will of any human person, but is given by God *through* people, as they were "carried along by the Holy Spirit"[101]. Peter is speaking in this passage about 'the prophesy of Scripture', which refers to the divine inspiration of the Bible, but the process of bringing about prophesy that *isn't* Scripture is done through the same process; God speaks through people.

In his letter to the Galatian church, Paul explains to them that the Spirit they received after hearing with faith is the Spirit who works miracles among them[102]; the miracles they are seeing in their midst are the result of the Spirit being in their midst. Furthermore, we have already discussed in chapter 2 the passage in Hebrews 2, which explains that God bore witness to the readers of this letter by "signs and wonders and various miracles and by gifts of the Holy Spirit"[103]. The writer to the Hebrews explains that these miracles, signs, wonders and gifts were given as a witness to the gospel of Jesus Christ; who can disagree that the gospel needs to be proclaimed in any way that God sees fit, especially when this passage says that the gifts, miracles and signs and wonders are "distributed according to his will"[104]?

---

[100] 1 Corinthians 14:33
[101] 2 Peter 1:21
[102] Galatians 3:5
[103] Hebrews 2:4
[104] Hebrews 2:4

## The Spirit is a gift

One of the criteria for something being a gift is that it is distributed according to the will of the person giving it. Or to put it another way, the giver gets to decide what is given. If I give my wife a gift, I get to choose what that gift will be. In a similar way, the gifts of the Spirit are given in a way that God sees best fit. We have seen that every Christian is the recipient of gifts of the Spirit, but that these gifts will vary from person to person. However, we are instructed by Scripture to seek the gifts, especially prophesy. This means that we cannot adopt a fatalistic approach to spiritual gifts. Yes, they are given according to the will of God, and yes they are to be sought. We must find the tension between these two truths, and not lean too strongly one way or the other.

However, there is a different way to look at God's generous giving of the Holy Spirit, which is that the very person of the Holy Spirit is Himself a gift. Jesus explains this in Luke 11, where he asks, hypothetically, which Father would give his son a scorpion when he was asked for an egg[105]. He then asks if human fathers, who compared to Father God are evil, know how to give good gifts to their children, "how much more will the heavenly Father give the Holy Spirit to those who ask him!"[106] Jesus regarded the Holy Spirit as a gift given by a good Father to His beloved children. In John's gospel, Jesus declares at the end of the Feast of Booths that if anyone who thirsts should come to Him and drink, and that out of that person's heart would flow rivers of living water. John notes that Jesus was speaking about the Spirit, who, at this point, had not yet been given because Jesus had not yet been glorified[107]. John is very much of the view that the Spirit was a gift, which would be given to the church after Jesus had been crucified, resurrected and glorified. After the resurrection, Jesus commissions the disciples and sends

---

[105] Luke 11:12
[106] Luke 11:13
[107] John 7:37-29

them as the Father had sent Him. He does this by breathing on them, saying "receive the Holy Spirit"[108]. The implication from John's gospel is that the Holy Spirit is a gift given by Jesus and the Father to the church.

We have already discussed Peter's sermon at Pentecost, but he is of a similar point of view. In addition to being convinced that the gifts being manifested by the church were *from* the Holy Spirit, Peter also urges the gathered crowd to repent, be baptized and to receive gift *of* the Holy Spirit[109]. Peter makes the distinction between the gift of the Spirit Himself, and gifts that the Spirit brings. When he and the other apostles are on trial, their defence to the high priest as to why they cannot stop speaking about Jesus is that they are witnesses of Jesus' life, death and resurrection, and so is the Holy Spirit, "whom God has given to those who obey Him"[110]. Later, Peter and John go down to pray with the disciples in Samaria 'that they might receive the Holy Spirit'[111]. Later still, when discussing the conversion of the gentiles, Peter declares that the Spirit has been given as a gift to Jew and gentile alike, thus erasing the outdated social distinctions which the Pharisees were trying to impose[112]. Luke, the author of Acts, was well aware of the gifts of the Holy Spirit, as we have explored above, and yet does not see a difficulty in describing the Holy Spirit Himself as someone to be received, and not just to receive the gifts He brings. A poor analogy would be of a parent giving gifts to His children. The gifts are pleasant, and might indeed be valuable, but the parent in our analogy is looking to be received as someone more than just the bringer of gifts. In the same way, the Holy Spirit is indeed the bringer of gifts, but is also someone to be received in His own right.

---

[108] John 20:22
[109] Acts 2:38
[110] Acts 5:32
[111] Acts 8:15
[112] Acts 15:8

Paul uses very strong language in his letter to the Galatian church, rebuking them for being tempted to return to the law for their salvation. 'O foolish Galatians!' he proclaims, then asking them whether they received the Spirit by works or by faith[113]. The obvious answer is that they received the Spirit as a gift; no one could work for their salvation and so no one could work in order to receive the Spirit. Paul explains that through what Jesus has done on the cross, they can receive the promised Spirit through faith[114], not through works of the law. Using similarly strong language, Paul urges the Thessalonian church to abandon their sexually immoral ways and to control their bodies in holiness and honour. He warns them that if they disregard this instruction, they are not ignoring the command of a man, but the command of God, "who gives His Holy Spirit to [them]"[115]. The implication given here is that to continually disregard God's way of living has a correlation with the gift of the Holy Spirit. Paul does not overtly say that if they don't stop sleeping around that God will remove His Spirit from them, but there is certainly a connection between a person's lifestyle and the ministry of the Spirit in their life.

Paul writes along the same lines in 1 Corinthians 6, asking; "Shall I then take the members of Christ and make them members of a prostitute? Never! ... Do you not know that your body is a temple of the Holy Spirit within you, whom you have from God?"[116] What we do with our bodies is linked with the role of the Holy Spirit within us. Akin to this reasoning, John writes that whoever keeps Christ's commandments abides in God, and God in him, and we know this because of the Holy Spirit whom has been given to us[117]. This is not to say that keeping commandments gains us the Spirit, rather the other way around; having the Spirit enables us to keep the

---

[113] Galatians 3:2
[114] Galatians 3:14
[115] 1 Thessalonians 4:8
[116] 1 Corinthians 6:15,19
[117] 1 John 3:24, 1 John 4:13

commandments. The Holy Spirit Himself is a heavenly gift[118], a helper given to enable Christians to live holy lives and to know that they abide in God and God abides in them. We cannot do without this gift.

## Conclusions

What can we conclude from these considerations? We first of all should conclude that any gifts given by the Holy Spirit are given in order to bring glory to God. This was the case in both the Old and New Testaments, and is still the case today. This means that if someone is using a gift in a way which does not bring glory to God, then this would not be a Biblical way to use this gift. That is not to say that the person is a fraud, or that they should not use that gift at all, but rather that they should be made aware that the gifts are given to glorify God.

Secondly, we should steer away from any view or teaching which says that gifts are only given to special people. We might well conclude that this teaching was correct if we were just to read the Old Testament, but the wealth of teaching in the New Testament shows that the gifts are given to the whole church, not just an elect or select part of it. This means that we should cultivate an environment where people feel safe, secure and enabled in their gifting, regardless of what that gifting is and regardless of how I might *feel* about such a gifting. If it's in the Bible, it should be welcomed in the church. This means not settling for the providential view of God that He will do what He wants when He wants to do it. This of course is true, but we are urged over and over again by Paul, Jesus and Luke to seek the gifts, to implore God for the gifts and to greatly desire the gifts.

Finally, because the Bible teaches that the Spirit both brings gifts and is a gift Himself, we should personally welcome the Spirit into our churches. We should develop theologies which emphasise the

---

[118] Hebrews 6:4

divinity of the Spirit; that He is a person to be valued and not just the means to an end in bringing gifts. What we do is often a result of what we say and believe, and as such we must speak highly of the Holy Spirit and not treat Him as some divine butler who brings gifts to the table but is Himself not invited to sit and eat.

# Four

# The Spirit Empowers, Enables and Equips God's People

## ✳✳✳

In the last chapter, we explored the gifts that the Holy Spirit gives. However, as we read the Bible we find that the work of the Holy Spirit is broader than this alone. We find that while the Spirit *does* bring gifts, He also empowers, enables and equips God's people in a bigger sense to fulfil His plans and purposes. If we invite the Holy Spirit into our churches and into our lives, we should expect there to be some sort of difference because He is present[119]. In this chapter we will explore what the Bible has to say about the Spirit empowering, enabling and equipping God's people.

### The Old Testament

The first instance of this is found in Genesis 41, where Joseph correctly and remarkably interprets the troubling dreams of the Egyptian Pharaoh. Although Joseph was a prisoner in jail on a falsified rape charge, he so astounds the leader of the most powerful nation on the planet that he is immediately exonerated and given power over the whole land. Pharaoh, who was popularly believed to be a deity himself, exclaims "Can we find a man like this, in whom is the Spirit of God?"[120] The Spirit enabled Joseph to correctly interpret

---

[119] Of course, when I am speaking about the Holy Spirit being present in our churches, I am not implying that He is absent from non-charismatic churches. All churches who confess Jesus as Lord have the Holy Spirit. Rather, I am referring to the intentional seeking of the Holy Spirit and His presence instead of accepting the truth of His 'general presence' covering the earth.

a prophetic dream, interestingly given by God to a pagan leader, in order to get Joseph out of prison as well as to save the lives of millions of people who would otherwise have died of famine. Joseph engineers this, and in the process is reunited with his murderous brothers and grieving father. We know that their descendants would be enslaved for almost half a millennia, but God would appoint Moses to lead them out of slavery and into their own theocratic land.

We read in Numbers 11 that Moses, an elderly man charged with the physical, emotional, legal and spiritual care of a few million people, is at breaking point with the people and gives God an ultimatum;

> "I am not able to carry all this people alone; the burden is too heavy for me. If you will treat me like this, kill me at once, if I find favour in your sight."[121]

Moses tells God either to get him some help, or else to just kill him. He was refusing to carry on alone. We might well ask why, if God is omniscient, did He not instruct Moses to appoint helpers because the burden was getting too heavy? I believe the answer to this question is that God is seeking a relationship with us, and He wants His people to rely on Him. Moses had done a great task of leading the Israelites to freedom. Their journey should have taken them less than three weeks, but because of their disobedience it was taking them much longer than that. God wanted Moses to rely on Him when the circumstances changed, rather than clinging to the previous set of edicts.

God listens to Moses' request, and tells him to gather seventy elders and to meet Him in the tent of meeting. God then "takes some of the Spirit that is on [Moses] and put it on [the seventy elders]"[122], so that they could bear the burden of leading the people along with Moses so he needn't do it alone. This verse tells us that the Spirit,

---

[120] Genesis 41:38
[121] Numbers 11:14-15
[122] Numbers 11:17, 25

who equipped Moses to lead the people, was then given to the seventy elders in order to equip them to do the same task. This is, of course, a spiritual happening, but it is also a practical and even legal necessity; the leaders of Israel at that time were responsible for leading the people in their relationship with God, but also in their relationship within each other in a society. Remember, no living Israelite for more than 400 years had been an autonomous person. In slavery, every one of them had been told when to sleep, when to work and when to eat, but now they had legal freedom from this oppression. They needed help in adjudicating legal disputes, and since all the leaders except Moses had also been slaves, they needed supernatural help to do this. The reformer Martin Luther wrote;

> "...the works of monks and priests... differ no whit in the sight of God from the works of the rustic toiling in the field or the woman going about her household tasks..."[123]

We are mistaken if we believe that only church leaders need the Spirit's help in order to fulfil their remit.

In the time of the judges, after Gideon destroys the alter of Baal in Judges 6, his father defused a death threat against Gideon by charging Baal, if he truly is a god, to contend for himself rather than having his followers do it for him. In the face of imminent battle, Scripture tells us that "The Spirit of the LORD clothed Gideon, and he sounded the trumpet"[124]. He then rallied several other tribes' armies and, after laying a fleece to make doubly sure he would triumph, defeated the Midianite army with only 300 men. Here we see the Spirit equipping Gideon with great courage in the face of ridiculous odds by covering him with Himself; Gideon knew intimately that the Spirit was with him.

---

[123] M. Luther, *'The Babylonian Captivity of the Church'*, Philadelphia Edition, 1520, Volume 2, p241
[124] Judges 6:34

Another of the judges, Jephthah, was similarly described as having "the Spirit of the LORD"[125] upon him, which enabled him to triumph over the Ammonites when previously he was unable to convince their king to listen to him. However, Jephthah made some poor and rash decisions immediately after he was described in this way. He vowed that, if God gave the Ammonites into his hand, the first person to emerge from his house and greet him upon his triumphant return would be sacrificed as a burnt offering to the LORD. That first person happened to be his daughter. This tragic circumstance shows us that being anointed by the Spirit of God does not automatically mean that every decision will turn out to be a good one. Even when we are anointed with the very Spirit of the living God, we still need to seek wise counsel and make sensible decisions; we cannot expect God's presence to over-ride our freedom to make decisions, either for good or for ill.

We have already discussed Samson in the previous chapter, but the Holy Spirit was involved in his life in more ways than giving him gifts. In the first verses where he is mentioned in the Bible, it says that "the LORD blessed him"[126], and that "the Spirit of the LORD began to stir him..."[127] While the Spirit of God was certainly bringing specific gifts and abilities to Samson, in each of the examples of the Spirit of God 'rushing upon' him, there is certainly an element of him being equipped and enabled to do super-human things with super-human strength. When he tears the lion to pieces barehanded[128], strikes down thirty men[129] and breaks the new ropes he was tied up with[130], the Spirit of God is upon him and empowered him to do these remarkable things. Equally, we have mentioned the messengers of Saul who were empowered with the Holy Spirit, and as a result

---

[125] Judges 11:29
[126] Judges 13:24
[127] Judges 13:25
[128] Judges 14:6
[129] Judges 14:19
[130] Judges 15:14

prophesied[131]. Empowering often results in the manifestation of specific gifts, but not always, as we shall see.

The Old Testament prophets had some experience of the empowering activity of God the Spirit. Isaiah, for example, prophesied about a time when the country would no longer be a desolate wasteland, as it was destined to be at the time he was prophesying, but rather that the wilderness will become a fruitful field, a pleasant forest[132]. This turn-around would cause 'justice [to] dwell in the wilderness, and righteousness [to] abide in the fruitful field', the result of which would be peace[133]. What was prophesied to be the catalyst for this miraculous happening? "The Spirit will be poured out from on high"[134]. The presence of the Spirit, and His being poured out from heaven, turns barren land to luscious springs and turns injustice into righteousness.

The Spirit is mentioned several times in Isaiah 63 too, as the prophet recounts the LORD's miraculous delivery of the Israelites from Egypt under Moses. The Spirit is described as having enabled Moses to split the Red Sea in order to create an everlasting name for the LORD[135], but in the very next breath the same Spirit is credited with having given the people of Israel rest, again to make a glorious name for the LORD[136]. This insight gives us a wonderful understanding of the diversity of the enabling power of the Spirit. He can equip a person with mighty miracles to lead millions of people on foot through a sea, and he can equally bring rest to those people when they need it. Isaiah sees no inconsistency in these two sides to the Spirit. Often, we can so readily put the Spirit into a box and say, in effect, 'He works like this; He doesn't work like that'. The fact is that the Spirit is far more diverse than we often give Him credit for.

---

[131] 1 Samuel 19:20
[132] Isaiah 32:14-15
[133] Isaiah 32:16-17
[134] Isaiah 32:15
[135] Isaiah 63:11
[136] Isaiah 63:14

Micah, in the book bearing his name, writes about being filled with the Spirit of God, justice and might, the combination of which equips him to proclaim to the nation of Israel their desolation and sin[137]. Similarly, Zechariah prophesies to Zerubbabel, the leader of one of the first groups of exiles to return from Babylon, that he will not prosper by might, or by power, but rather by the Spirit of the LORD[138] would he succeed in laying the foundations of the second temple. Zerubbabel presumably already had might and power, but these things would not get the job done; he needed to rely on that which God would supply, namely His Spirit. The final Old Testament reference to the Spirit empowering is in Malachi, where the Spirit is described as making two people in a marriage into one union[139]. The Spirit has a role in bringing two people into one marriage commitment, and each receives 'a portion of the Spirit in their union.'[140]

**The Gospels**

Moving into the New Testament, the wonderful character of John the Baptist[141] contrasts his ministry with that of Jesus, saying that he baptises with water for repentance, whereas Jesus "will baptise you with the Holy Spirit and with fire."[142] Mark and John's gospels also make reference to Jesus baptizing with the Holy Spirit[143], and Peter refers to it in Acts 11[144], but only Luke and Matthew's gospels make mention of being 'baptized with fire'[145]. There are several ways to

---

[137] Micah 3:8
[138] Zechariah 4:6
[139] Malachi 2:15
[140] Malachi 2:15
[141] The correct reading of his name and title in Matthew 3 (and elsewhere) would be 'John the Baptizer', that being, 'John who dips into water'. Calling him 'John the Baptist' implies that he was the founder or support of a particular Christian denomination, but for the sake of clarity I have used his more commonly known name.
[142] Matthew 3:11
[143] Mark 1:8, John 1:33
[144] Acts 11:16

understand what is meant by 'fire'. The Greek word here is '*pyr*', from which we get our words 'pyrotechnic' and 'pyromaniac'. This word has no other meaning in Scripture other than 'fire', and, if it were to be a metaphor for something, it would be the context of the passage that would make it so. An obvious connection between these verses concerning the Holy Spirit and fire is with Acts 2:3, where the Holy Spirit falls on the church on the day of Pentecost and "tongues as of fire appeared to them and rested on each one of them".

However, if Acts 2:3 is the only example of what John the Baptist said in Matthew 3, it would seem like a very narrow fulfilment of 'baptised with fire', as Acts 2:3 is the only time in Scripture when tongues of fire fell upon believers, while the baptism of the Spirit is mentioned many times. Why would John the Baptist, and Matthew who recorded his words, make such a mention of Jesus baptising 'with fire' when Pentecost was the only recorded occasion when this literally occurred, yet the baptism of the Spirit is an experience available to everyone?[146] Perhaps 'fire' in this instance is a reference to two prophecies in the Old Testament, which speak about the LORD cleansing His people with "a spirit of judgement and a spirit of burning"[147], and also of refining and purifying the people like a 'refiner's fire', so that they may bring offerings of righteousness to the LORD[148]. If this is the correct interpretation, it would shed some light on what the Spirit did on the day of Pentecost. The 'fire' of the Holy Spirit is a refiners fire, which strips away that which is perishable and leaves that which is imperishable, so that the person who is being baptised can, as Malachi says, make offerings of

---

[145] Matthew 3:11, Luke 3:16

[146] A good rule-of-thumb for Biblical interpretation is to assume that if something happens once in the New Testament, then we shouldn't be surprised if it happens again in our contemporary church. If something happens in the New Testament more than once, we should *expect* it to happen in our contemporary church.

[147] Isaiah 4:4

[148] Malachi 3:2-3

righteousness to the LORD. In a New Testament context, this could be conviction of sin and turning to Jesus, or else a greater appreciation of God's glory and who He has made us to be through Jesus' sacrifice. Either way, the gospels say that it is Jesus who baptises with the Holy Spirit and with fire, and this experience yields a powerful ability to live for Him.

Matthew, Mark, Luke and John all specifically mention the Spirit descending on Jesus at His baptism, which was the beginning of His earthly ministry, while Matthew and John emphasise the fact that the Spirit 'rested upon Him', indicating that this wasn't a temporary empowering but rather an on-going partnership[149]. Mark makes the point that heaven was 'torn open' before the Holy Spirit descended, which presumably was in reference to the cry of the Old Testament peoples for God to come to them on earth[150]. Mark is clarifying for all his readers that this Jesus is God in the flesh; that God has come to earth to be with them.

Matthew, Mark and Luke all make reference to the Spirit descending on Jesus 'like a dove', but Luke's account has a variation, which describes the Spirit descending "in bodily form, like a dove"[151]. Luke, the meticulous doctor, makes the point that the Spirit descending on Jesus wasn't simply a marker at the beginning of his ministry, rather that there was a physical presence present upon Jesus when the Spirit descended. Why the gospel writers describe the Spirit as being 'like a dove' is a mystery. Some have hypothesized that the dove is the symbol of peace *because* the Spirit is the Spirit of peace[152], but this would be to reverse-engineer the symbol; the dove started being used as the symbol of peace because the Spirit is the Spirit of peace. Whatever the reason for His bird-like appearance, the Spirit, on this occasion and at no other time in Scripture, descended on Jesus in bodily form like a dove and remained on Him. After his time in the

---

[149] Matthew 3:16, John 1:33
[150] Isaiah 64:1, Psalm 144:5. Also see 2 Samuel 22:10 and Psalm 18:9
[151] Luke 3:22
[152] Romans 8:6, Romans 14:7, Galatians 5:22, Ephesians 4:3

wilderness, Jesus returns to Galilee "in the power of the Spirit" and began to teach and perform miracles[153]. Although Jesus was fully God, he waited until He had received the Spirit before He began to move in power.

**Acts**

If we were to summarise the content of Jesus' ministry, the single sentence 'Teaching, preaching, healing and performing miracles' would suffice. All four of these elements point us towards who Jesus is; Emmanuel, God with us. The first church in Acts knew and modelled this after Jesus assured them that, in order to go and be His witnesses from Jerusalem to the ends of the earth, they would "be baptized with the Holy Spirit"[154] and would "receive power"[155]. They wouldn't need to go and evangelise and witness in their own strength, something which Christians can all too easily stray into. Rather, Christ had a superior idea; 'Go in the power of the Spirit.' The first church had walked with Jesus in the flesh some for three years, and still needed the empowering presence of the Spirit; why should we, who have not heard the words of eternal life from His lips, be any different? This is outlined by the testimony of Acts 4, which tells that after Peter and John had been hauled before the council, the church was praying for boldness. Luke says that "they were all filled with the Holy Spirit and continued to speak the word of God with boldness"[156]. Notice that this is not Pentecost, but rather was a subsequent event. The church was continually seeking to encounter the Holy Spirit, the result of which was that they proclaimed the word of God boldly.

Later, when the apostles heard that Samaria had responded to the gospel, they dispatch Peter and John to pray with the new believers that they would receive the Holy Spirit, because they had *only* been

---

[153] Luke 4:14, 15, 31
[154] Acts 1:5
[155] Acts 1:8
[156] Acts 4:31

baptised into the name of Jesus. This is an important distinction, which we will explore in chapter 8, but Peter and John thought it important to go to Samaria and lay hands on them so that they might receive the Holy Spirit[157]. They clearly still had in mind the words of Jesus, "...you will receive power when the Holy Spirit has come upon you, and you will be my witnesses"[158]. They wanted to make sure that the newly founded church in Samaria was empowered to be Christ's witnesses by receiving the Holy Spirit.

The classic Calvinist, who believes in the sovereignty of God as the central factor of the Christian life, will question why the apostles needed to travel from Jerusalem to Samaria in order for the church to receive the Holy Spirit. What was the purpose of the laying on of hands? Could God, in His infinite power and wisdom, not make the receipt of the Holy Spirit an automatic event that happens at conversion? Yes, He could. However, this line of thinking both conveniently avoids the authority of Scripture (as it's in the Bible, so it must be God's preferred method), but also underplays the necessity of community, as well as the requirement for the Holy Spirit to be desired in the life of the believer[159]. Perhaps the Samarian church didn't know about the Holy Spirit, like the Ephesian church[160]. Or perhaps, even if they did know about the Holy Spirit, they didn't know how to receive Him, and so they needed some more experienced apostles to guide them. The laying on of hands, in some way, was the natural response to the apostles' desire to impart the Holy Spirit, and the power He brings, to the new Samarian believers.

---

[157] Acts 8:17

[158] Acts 1:8

[159] By this, I mean that the believer must *want* the Holy Spirit to empower their life, in the same way that the believer must *want* Jesus to be LORD of their life. These things are not automatic, but rather are the outcome of a growing relationship with the triune God.

[160] Acts 19:2

There is another interesting twist to the saga of the Samarian church. A magician named Simon was watching the apostles lay on hands, and he proposed to buy the Holy Spirit from them, so that he could give other people the power he had seen[161]. This offer was not met favourably. Peter deplores him for even suggesting that the Spirit is a commodity to be bought and sold, and commands that Simon repents, so that "the intent of [his] heart may be forgiven [him]"[162]. Simon quickly repents, but we are not explicitly told what the intent of his heart was. However, it seems that Peter rebuked him so immediately and so strongly because by offering money for the Holy Spirit, who is both God *and* a gift of God, Simon was proposing to purchase God. Someone who purchases something owns it, and may use it as he sees fit. Someone who is given something as a gift in trust is answerable to the one who gave it. In the case of the Holy Spirit, God is both the giver and the gift, and so Simon's desire to own the Holy Spirit shows us that his heart was not for God and his glory, but for something else; be it power before people, wealth by selling the Holy Spirit to others, or the praises of men. The Holy Spirit does not dance to our tune. Rather, He provides the music.

## Paul's letters

The apostle Paul had much to say about the Spirit equipping, enabling and empowering believers. The book of Romans is the setting for a battleground upon which Paul pits living by the flesh against living by the Spirit. The opening words of Romans explains, with amazing clarity, exactly who Jesus is. Paul both proclaims the truth about Jesus' deity and His humanity, saying that Jesus was,

> "...descended from David according to the flesh and was declared to be the Son of God in power according to the Spirit of holiness by his resurrection from the dead..."[163]

---

[161] Acts 8:19
[162] Acts 8:22
[163] Romans 1:4

By this amazing opening, Paul is telling us that though Jesus was fully human, just as we are, He also had amazing 'power according to the Spirit of holiness'. Is this not a beautiful description of Jesus' character? 'Power and holiness'. If we believe that Jesus was really human, and if we are to emulate Jesus, then the power which enabled Him to do miracles is from the same Spirit who empowers us. But the Spirit is also the Spirit of holiness. All too often we can embrace the fruit of the Spirit[164] and ignore the gifts, or else embrace the gifts of the Spirit at the expense of the fruit. Both are given by the Spirit and both are empowering, but the product of each must be accompanied by the product of the other; Prophesy with kindness, teaching with patience, tongues with self-control. We must seek both the fruit and the gifts; anything less is shy of Jesus' model for us.

Paul mentions the enabling power of the Spirit six more times in Romans alone, and several times in Galatians. He speaks of Christ fulfilling the righteousness required by the law, and His impartation of that righteousness to us so that we may walk not according to the flesh, and therefore gratify its desires[165], but be led[166] and walk according to the Spirit[167]. The result of this is that those who live according to the Spirit will set their minds on the things of the Spirit.[168] Paul explains that setting your mind on the things of the flesh leads to death, because the desires of the flesh and the desires of the Spirit are against one another[169], but we are to set our minds on the Spirit, which brings life and peace[170]. This is underlined only a few verses later, when he says that living according to the flesh will kill you, but if you put the deeds of the flesh to death by the Spirit, you will live[171]. Paul is speaking about more than just material life and

---

[164] Galatians 5:22
[165] Galatians 5:16
[166] Galatians 5:18
[167] Romans 8:4, Galatians 5:25
[168] Romans 8:5
[169] Galatians 5:17
[170] Romans 8:6

death, because, as the psalmists observe, sometimes virtuous people die and evil people prosper[172]. Rather, what Paul is describing here is life *according to* the flesh, that being, believing and living like the material is all there is and denying the spiritual. Equally, the life and death Paul is talking about is eternal life and eternal death, essentially, heaven and hell. He is urging his readers to rely on the Spirit as the fuel of their lives, when we are strong, when we are weak and when we don't know how to pray[173]. This sentiment is echoed in Ephesians 6, where Paul urges his readers to "pray at all times in the Spirit", leaning on the Spirit's power when they pray[174]. Towards the end of Romans, Paul writes a prayer for them;

> "May the God of hope fill you with all joy and peace in believing, so that by the power of the Holy Spirit you may abound in hope."[175]

Paul is praying that by the power of the Spirit, his readers and we might abound in hope, joy and peace. The Spirit brings power, so that we might have hope, joy and peace in believing in Jesus. Equally, the Galatian churches are urged to eagerly await the hope of righteousness, "through the Spirit, by faith"[176], and Paul writes to the Ephesians that they might be equipped with power "through His Spirit in [their] inner beings"[177]. In 1 Corinthians, Paul also speaks about the power of the Holy Spirit in the life of the believer. When listing the gifts of the Spirit in chapter 12, Paul highlights the fact that the same Spirit gives each of these gifts[178]; no one gift can claim to be of loftier stock or of more importance than any other, because they are all of the same origin. These gifts testify to the

---

[171] Romans 8:13
[172] Psalm 73:2-16, 37:7, 92:7, et al.
[173] Romans 8:26
[174] Ephesians 6:18
[175] Romans 15:13
[176] Galatians 5:5
[177] Ephesians 3:16
[178] 1 Corinthians 12:11

authenticity of a ministry, certainly that of an apostle, as Paul makes clear in 1 Corinthians 2, where he says that his message was not of plausible words, but a demonstration of the Spirit and of power[179]. Paul's ministry was built on these demonstrations so that the Corinthians would not trust in human wisdom, but in God[180]. Should we also not strive to make the ministries of our church dependent on God and not on our own plausible words, however theologically accurate these may be? There is, of course, a great platform for apologetics, which we will explore in the next chapter, but, as we have seen, the enabling and equipping power of the Spirit is an absolute necessity for the Christian church. It was in the first century and it still is in the twenty-first century.

What, then, should we seek to do in response to this? Firstly, I believe that when a church is undertaking any ministry, God's favour, power and perspective should be perpetually sought. We do not have to do much research before finding a church, mission organisation or method of evangelism which was very clearly anointed by God at a particular time, but once they had begun to see some fruit, simply carried on with what they had been doing before. Those in charge stopped seeking God about their ministry, and as such the ministry methods they employed ceased to be effective as times and attitudes changed. Had they sought God incessantly, they may have clung less to past methods and been more open to new revelation. Work done by the church for the glory of God will be insurmountably more effective if we rely on what God has provided, namely, Himself. The Christian, and therefore the Church, is the temple of God, where God dwells on the earth. The Spirit empowers the Church to glorify God.

Secondly, the Holy Spirit is contextual. This does not mean that people are free to choose to include Him in their lives and churches or not as they see fit – they do so at their peril – rather, the Spirit is

---

[179] 1 Corinthians 2:4
[180] 1 Corinthians 2:5

way more diverse than we expect Him to be. He is God, and as such we cannot box the Spirit into our constraints and expectations. Adrian Plass, the satirical Christian author, once wrote of a fictitious church who wanted to arrange spontaneous worship so that it happened in the same time and in the same way every week[181]. Is it not true that we often wish to 'arrange' for the Spirit to empower us in a manner which we 'see fit'? We often wish to box the Spirit into being a particular way, either within our worship services, our creeds and mission statements, or else with our preaching and teaching. But as we have seen, the same Spirit who gives power to one person gives rest to the next. In response to this, let us pray, and really mean it, for the Spirit to equip us in whatever way *He sees fit.* As U2 sang on their 2004 album 'How to Dismantle an Atomic Bomb', "I want the lot of what you've got, and I want nothing that you're not."[182]

Finally, if we seek to be empowered, enabled and equipped by the Spirit of the living God, we must wield that power wisely. I believe that the fruit of the Spirit in Galatians 5 is given as guidelines for using the gifts of the Spirit in 1 Corinthians 12, and elsewhere. The gifts of the Spirit, including miracles, healings and signs and wonders are powerful tools, not to be used lightly, glibly or selfishly. Those moving in the power of the Spirit should equally seek His fruit. As Spider-man's uncle told him in their last conversation, "With great power comes great responsibility."[183]

---

[181] A. Plass, *'The Theatrical Tapes of Leonard Thynn'*, London: Marshall Pickering, 1989, p1

[182] U2, "Original of the Species", How to Dismantle an Atomic Bomb, Island Records, 2004

[183] Spiderman, 2002. Film. Directed by Sam RAIMI. USA: Columbia Pictures

# Five

# The Spirit Reveals and Empowers Teaching and Preaching

### \*\*\*

While it is my intention to be as thorough as possible in each chapter regarding the various activities of the Holy Spirit, the way I have structured these chapters means that we may only focus on one action at a time. Fear not, however! My objective is to take account of every single reference to the Spirit in Scripture, and to present them in a cohesive way. In the previous chapter, I made no reference to the Spirit revealing anything to God's people, which would of course equip them, nor to preaching and teaching, which empowers both the speaker and the hearers. My reason for omitting these elements of the Spirit's work is because they warranted a chapter unto themselves.

The late John Stott wrote of Charles Haddon Spurgeon that on his way up to the pulpit to preach, Spurgeon would whisper a prayer along the lines of, "I believe in the Holy Ghost, I believe in the Holy Ghost, I believe in the Holy Ghost."[184] Apart from an absolute cessationist, there are few who would not attribute preaching and teaching to the work of the Holy Spirit. While, as we have already seen, there is much more to the Holy Spirit than the application of God's Word to our hearts, souls and lives, we cannot overlook the wealth of Biblical weight behind this conviction. Neither can we ignore the many places in Scripture where the Holy Spirit reveals a specific piece of information to a person or group, quite independently of any preaching or teaching.

---

[184] J. R. W. Stott, *'The Preacher's Portrait'*, Michigan: Eerdmans Publishing, 1961, page 118

## Old Testament

Admittedly, there are very few examples of the Spirit revealing anything or empowering teaching and preaching[185] in the Old Testament. The first example is found in Nehemiah, where, in response to the reading of the law, the Levites (and others) are regaling the assembled people with a history of God's faithfulness. They summarize much of the Pentateuch, but when describing Israel's exodus from Egypt, they explain that, "[God] gave [His] good Spirit to instruct them"[186]. We have described in previous chapters the miraculous hand of God in bringing the Israelites out of slavery, but this reference adds a different perspective on the event; the Spirit was given to instruct them. This is one of His roles, to instruct God's people to follow God's ways.

The author of the 143rd psalm similarly expressed this, beseeching God to teach him to do His will, and to let His 'good Spirit' led him on level ground[187]. In Old Testament poetry, particularly in the psalms, the human author will sometimes express the same idea in two different ways. This is the case here; the psalmist is asking God to teach him, and asking the Spirit to lead him on level ground. He is equating the teaching of the Spirit with walking on level ground.

Three Old Testament prophets also reflected upon the teaching nature of the Spirit of God. Isaiah, when talking about the coming of the Messiah, describes how the Spirit will be with Him;

---

[185] There is an on-going debate as to the difference between 'teaching' and 'preaching'. To clarify our terms, I understand 'teaching' to be the explaining and applying of God's word to a group of believers, and I understand 'preaching' to be the presenting of the Gospel to unbelievers. I am aware that these terms are often used interchangeably, but, as we shall see, they are also used distinctively by the gospel writers and Paul.

[186] Nehemiah 9:20

[187] Psalm 143:10

"And the Spirit of the LORD shall rest upon him, the Spirit of wisdom and understanding, the Spirit of counsel and might, the Spirit of knowledge and the fear of the LORD."[188]

The Spirit of wisdom, understanding, counsel and knowledge will rest upon the Christ, and from where we sit in time the Spirit *has* rested upon Christ, and has equally has been made available to us. These qualities are a part of who the Holy Spirit is, and as such we should expect these qualities to be among the fruit of those who encounter Him regularly.

Ezekiel wrote that there will be a time, again pointing to the future from when it was written, when God will give believers a new heart and a new spirit[189], which will cause them to "walk in [His] statutes and be careful to obey [His] rules"[190]. The new Spirit being put into the hearts of believers reveals God in a more profound way than mere obedience to an external law. The Spirit reveals God's heart behind the laws, and thus empowers the believer to live in relationship with Him and love His ways. Zechariah writes along the same lines when he says that the people made their hearts diamond hard, "lest they should hear the law and the words that the LORD of hosts had sent by his Spirit through the former prophets"[191]. The Spirit's relationship with the prophets was to prompt, guide and inspire them. We will cover the inspiring work of the Spirit more fully in chapter 11, but we can safely say that the Spirit revealed the law and the words of the LORD to the people by His prophets in the Old Testament.

**The Gospels and Acts**

The Gospel writer Luke describes a man named Simeon who was righteous and devout, waiting for the "consolation of Israel"[192], that

---

[188] Isaiah 11:2
[189] Ezekiel 36:26
[190] Ezekiel 36:27
[191] Zechariah 7:12

being, the coming of Jesus. Luke records that Simeon had been 'told by the Holy Spirit' that he would live to see the Christ[193]. This was not given by a word of Scripture or prophesy, but rather Simeon apparently 'just knew' that this would be the case because the Spirit had revealed it to him. Information revealed by the Spirit will always come true, and should be weighed against Scripture[194]. As I have said, this occurrence is not prophesy, and so while it technically falls outside the instructions given in 1 Corinthians 14 and 1 John 4, we should remember that prophesy is essentially God giving information to person A for the benefit of person B. In this scenario, Scripture attests to the fact that the Holy Spirit revealed this information to Simeon; God gave this information to person A for the benefit of person A.

When Jesus was teaching his disciples and a vast crowd, He explained to them that their following Him would result in their being hauled before the rulers of synagogues and before the authorities. He tells them not to worry about what to say in their defence when that happens, for, "the Holy Spirit will teach you in that very hour what you ought to say."[195] At the last supper when Jesus was teaching His disciples about things to come, He explains about whom the Holy Spirit is and what He will do. Jesus describes the Spirit as "the Spirit of truth", who dwells with them[196]. Jesus goes on to explain that the Spirit will teach them all things, and bring to mind all the things that Jesus had taught them[197]. Notice that the text doesn't say that the Spirit will teach them all *Biblical* things, or all *spiritual* things, but rather the Spirit will teach them *all* things. The Holy Spirit is the teacher who teaches all things because the Spirit is omniscient; He knows all things. Equally as importantly, the Spirit brings the words and ways of Jesus to the minds of believers.

---

[192] Luke 2:25
[193] Luke 2:26
[194] 1 Corinthians 14:29, 1 John 4:1
[195] Luke 12:12
[196] John 14:17
[197] John 14:26

Both of these qualities are backed up by what Jesus goes on to say in the following chapters. John 15 has Jesus explaining that He will send the Spirit from the Father, that the Spirit is the Spirit of truth, and that the Spirit will bear witness about Him. This makes sense, as if Jesus is the way, the truth and the life[198], it would logically follow that He who bears witness about Jesus would be the Spirit of truth. John would later write that it is the Spirit who testifies, because the Spirit is the truth[199], but in the next chapter of his gospel, John recounts Jesus' explanation that "when the Spirit of Truth comes, He will guide you into all the truth"[200]. This is how the English Standard Version and the New International Version render this verse, however the King James Version doesn't include the word 'the' before 'truth'. This makes the verse read slightly differently, because if the Spirit guides us into 'all the truth', this implies that there is a specific truth which the Spirit guides us into, which given the context, would be the truth about Jesus. This would be an accurate statement.

However, the KJV's version omits the 'the', making the sentence read, 'guide you into all truth'. This opens up the scope of what truth the Spirit will guide us into, from 'truth about Jesus' to 'truth about all things'. The Greek in this passage does include the definite article 'the', but not in the way the ESV renders it. The Greek of this passage literally reads "that one the Spirit of the truth it shall be way leading you into every the truth."[201] So, it would seem that given this, along with Jesus' statement in John 14:26, that the proper reading of this verse would be 'When the Spirit of truth comes, he will guide you into all truth'. This means that the Spirit does indeed guide us into the truth about Jesus, His work is certainly not less than this, but also guides into *all* truth. According to this logic, whenever something is written or thought about which is true, it was

---

198 John 14:6
199 1 John 5:6
200 John 16:13
201 http://www.scripture4all.org/OnlineInterlinear/NTpdf/joh16.pdf

the Spirit of God who revealed that truth to that person. This widens the scope of how we should understand the work of the Spirit from 'truth in the church' to 'truth wherever a Christian is'; the Spirit can bring truth about business, agriculture and academia just as much as He can bring truth about Christ.

When Jesus promised His disciples that they would be hauled in front of councils and made to defend themselves, I wonder how many of them believed it would actually happen. If they didn't believe it before Jesus' resurrection and ascension, they began to believe it soon afterwards! Acts 4 records that for the 'crime' of healing a lame beggar, Peter and John are required to answer to the rulers, elders, scribes, the high priest and the high priest's family[202]. However, just as Jesus said would happen in Luke 12, "Peter, filled with the Holy Spirit,"[203] explained to them that the good deed done to the crippled man was done by the name of Jesus.

This instance of the Spirit giving Peter the words to say in a tough situation shows one side of the Spirit's revealing powers. Peter experiences another side of these powers just after his rooftop vision in Acts 10, where "the Spirit said to him, "Behold, three men are looking for you. Rise and go down and accompany them without hesitation, for I have sent them".[204] Here, the Spirit speaks directly to Peter for the simple reason of communicating with him after he'd had an intense spiritual encounter. The Spirit was prompting Peter onto the next phase of his journey as a messianic Jew; he's been profoundly told off by 'the voice' for calling certain animals unclean when both God and Christ had declared them to be clean[205]. The Spirit, talking to him in this way, was to turn his encounter into action, that being to bring the gospel to the gentiles in Caesarea and so break down the barriers between Jew and gentile.

---

[202] Acts 4:5
[203] Acts 4:8
[204] Acts 10:19-20
[205] Mark 7:18-19

## The Epistles and Revelation

Paul, the self-confessed expert in the law who therefore presumably knew the Old Testament backwards and forwards, writes almost casually in Romans 8 that "The Spirit himself bears witness with our spirit that we are children of God"[206]. Considering that we read in John 5 that the Jews were seeking to kill Jesus for calling God his Father[207], this is a bold statement. The Holy Spirit shares with our spirit, with our inner person, that we are children of God. This phrase translated here as 'bearing witness' occurs only four times in the New Testament, three of which are in Romans. The Greek word for this phrase is 'symmartyreo', and is used in Revelation, translated as 'to testify'[208]. This helps to shed some light on a somewhat strange expression. The Spirit communicates something to us about our status as sons and daughters of God. There is another word which means 'to be a witness of something', which is 'martyreo', from which we get our word 'martyr', but 'symmartyreo' has a broader meaning incorporating an element of divine revelation within the word itself.

However, this reference in Romans 8 is more than the simple passing on of information, because, as the previous verse tells us, we have received adoption as God's children through the Spirit, and our response to this adoption is to cry out "Abba, Father!"[209] Our being God's children is much more than a legal transaction, it is a heart-cry of a child to a loving parent. When my two-year-old son wants my attention, his attempts to get this aren't reasoned and calculated. Rather, he shouts, waves his hands around and runs towards me laughing and giggling when he wants me. As his father, his desire for a cuddle warms my heart, and it is a joy to shower him with affection. This is what the Spirit causes us to feel towards God

---

[206] Romans 8:16
[207] John 5:18
[208] Revelation 22:18
[209] Romans 8:15

the Father; 'Abba' is an affectionate term for God, by which Jesus addresses Him in an intimate moment of prayer[210]. This is the phrase which the Spirit causes us to utter towards our heavenly Dad.

We also find this phrase 'the Spirit bears witness' in Romans 9, where Paul, just before he tells the Roman church of his great sorrow and anguish for their salvation, assures his readers that what he is about to say is true. As evidence for this, he points to his conscience, which he says "bears [him] witness in the Holy Spirit"[211]. We see here that the Holy Spirit once again agrees with a part of us, and the union of these two elements means that the issue in question is true and right and trustworthy. God has given us a conscience in order to determine right from wrong. However, our consciences may be misled, and so we need to join with the Spirit of truth to determine what the right course of action is. The Spirit will not contradict Himself, so if several people seek Him about the right thing to do, the correct way will emerge. Perhaps this is a preferential way of seeking the future of a church than a show of hands?

The writer to the Hebrews describes how the Holy Spirit affirms that the transition from the old covenant to the new covenant has indeed happened, and refers to Jeremiah 31 as proof of this[212]. When the Spirit affirms that something is true, it most certainly is true. Paul alludes to this in 1 Corinthians 2, when he refers to the Spirit revealing the truth about;

> "What no eye has seen, nor ear heard, nor the heart of man imagined, what God has prepared for those who love him."[213]

---

[210] Mark 14:36
[211] Romans 9:1
[212] Hebrews 10:15
[213] 1 Corinthians 2:9

This is a paraphrase of Isaiah 64:4 and Paul is saying here that the Spirit has revealed to him information about the things that God has prepared for those who love Him. These things are not deducible by the eye, ear or heart of men, because they are revealed by the very heart of God to those whose hearts are towards Him. This verse explains why this is the case, saying that "the Spirit searches everything, even the depths of God"[214]. The Spirit accesses the depths of God and helps us understand things we could never learn on our own. This Spirit is of God, not of the world, and is given so that we might understand the things of God which He has given us.[215] Along with empowering those who preach and teach, which is mentioned relatively rarely in Scripture, the Holy Spirit himself is our teacher about the things of God. This can certainly be by the medium of a preacher, but more frequently it is through a direct divine revelation. Paul happily marries these two ideas when he says that he "[imparts] this in words not taught by human wisdom but taught by the Spirit."[216] He received wisdom from the Spirit, who illuminates Scripture, and imparts it to others by the Spirit. Paul gives us another example of this in 1 Timothy 4, where he relays to Timothy what the Spirit has said, namely that some will depart from the faith "in later times"[217].

Similarly, the writer to the Hebrews explains that during the time when the 'first section' of the temple was still standing, the way into the holy place was not accessible[218]. The writer is making a comparison between where most people were allowed and where only the high priest was allowed, and how, in Christ, those divisions are done away with. But the writer points to the Holy Spirit, who 'indicates' that this is the correct interpretation of the old covenant

---

[214] 1 Corinthians 2:10
[215] 1 Corinthians 2:12
[216] 1 Corinthians 2:13
[217] 1 Timothy 4:1
[218] Hebrews 9:8

temple in light of a new covenant High Priest. The Spirit seems to have brought this point to the mind of the writer, revealing aspects and perspectives which might have otherwise gone unnoticed. Many of us who survey the Scriptures will resonate with this idea; the Spirit reveals truths to us which we have previously missed entirely.

As we have seen, the Spirit is heavily involved in the teaching done by the church, both in the bringing about of revelation to church leaders through Scripture and in the revealing of divine truth to individuals. However, sometimes the Spirit is less than clear about a certain subject, and apparently the individual must determine what the correct course of action is by seeking the Spirit's wisdom, and listening to their own conscience. An example of this is found in 1 Corinthians 7, where Paul is explaining how people should act regarding romantic relationships. He says in the first instance (in verse 39) that a wife is bound to her husband for as long as he lives. Then, he explains that if the husband dies, the wife is free to marry whoever she wants, provided he is a believer[219]. These two statements seem rather unequivocal, but then Paul goes on to say that, in his judgement, she is happier if she remains as she is, presumably meaning a widow. His basis for this is, "And I think that I too have the Spirit of God."[220] Either, Paul has just contradicted what he wrote in the previous verse, or else this second statement is his perspective, rather than a direct instruction. Paul in no way merely 'thought' that he had the Spirit of God; he spends too much time in 1 Corinthians, Ephesians, Romans and many other of his letters explaining how he and all Christians most certainly do have the Spirit. Rather, he seems almost timid in verse 40, as if he isn't entirely sure about the subject in hand, and is venturing an opinion as opposed to giving a direct teaching. Although this is a somewhat unclear part of Scripture, it does seem that Paul is leaving the matter open to the conscience of the individual believer.

---

[219] 1 Corinthians 7:39
[220] 1 Corinthians 7:40

In his first letter, John writes that we are to test the spirits to determine which ones are from God and which ones are not[221]. He explains that 'by this we know the Spirit of truth and the spirit of error'. What we must not assume is that everything that is 'spiritual' is necessarily good. Rather, we are instructed in this passage to test the spirits, the implication being that not all spirits are of God and therefore need to be rejected. The Spirit of truth will reveal to us which spirits are of God, and which aren't.

There is perhaps an example of the Spirit revealing something to Paul about another person. Paul writes to the Colossians that Epaphras was a faithful minister of Christ in their behalf[222], and "has made known to us your love in the Spirit"[223]. The phrasing of this verse is interesting, and could be read in several ways. One way to read it would be that Epaphras "has made known to us your love, in the Spirit." This would mean that the Spirit was the method by which Epaphras made known the Colossians' love to Paul. Another way to read this verse would be that Epaphras "has made known to us how much you love the Spirit", which would be a commendable feather in the Colossians cap. A final way to read this verse would be that Epaphras "has made known to us your love [for one another] in [the fellowship of] the Spirit". This reading would highlight the bond of fellowship provided by the Spirit. Because any punctuation used in an English translation has been inserted by the translators, we can read each of these renditions equally legitimately. However, could it not be so that this verse has several meanings? Could the Colossians not have had an outstanding degree of love for one another, by and in the Spirit? Would it be so unthinkable for the Spirit to have prompted Epaphras to share this with Paul, or else for Paul to 'sense the truth of their love' from Epaphras through the Spirit? The text is left open to interpretation.

---

[221] 1 John 4:1
[222] Colossians 1:7
[223] Colossians 1:8

The apostle Peter also gives us an interesting insight into the ministry of the Spirit, when he says that the Old Testament Prophets prophesied by 'the Spirit of Christ' when they predicted the sufferings of Christ and His subsequent glory[224]. Several aspects of this sentence are striking, firstly that Peter, Jesus' closest friend, refers to the Spirit as 'the Spirit of Christ'. If nothing else, this shows us that Peter recognized the 'fragrance' of Jesus' work and life in the work of the Spirit. In this passage, Peter is linking up the work of the Old Testament prophets with the work of the New Testament preachers. He explains, with remarkable insight, that the Old Testament prophets knew that they spoke not for their own benefits, but for the benefit of his readers, the church[225]. Peter here affirms the belief that it is by the Holy Spirit that the gospel is preached, and that angels long to explore it[226]. Although this is, certainly numerically, a relatively minor role of the Holy Spirit, we should not overlook it. Regardless of the differences in style and emphasis, most church services will contain some sort of sermon. Our preaching of God's word should be saturated with the Spirit of God, and we should rely on His guidance constantly in our preparation and delivery, because preaching is a heavenly activity[227].

The final book of the Bible also shows us something of how the Sprit teaches us. The apostle John, exiled to the rugged island of Patmos, has a profound encounter with the Risen Christ. Jesus tells John to write seven letters to various churches around what is now Turkey. Towards the end of each letter, Jesus uses a curious phrase, which is "He who has an ear, let him hear what the Spirit says to the churches"[228]. This is interesting for several reasons. Firstly, it means that although there are different issues being spoken about for the various churches, the Sprit is involved in speaking to each one. This

---

[224] 1 Peter 1:11
[225] 1 Peter 1:12
[226] 1 Peter 1:12
[227] 1 Peter 1:12
[228] Revelation 2:7, 2:11, 2:17, 2:29, 3:6, 3:13, 3:22

affirms the divine authorship of the book of Revelation by the Spirit. Secondly, the repeated use of this phrase closely links the work of Christ with the work of the Spirit, even after Jesus' resurrection and ascension. Notice that, in these passages, it is Jesus who is speaking to the churches, but He includes in each letter the phrase 'let him hear what *the Spirit* says to the churches.' Christ, just like Peter in 1 Peter 1, has no problem in identifying His words with the words of the Spirit. In effect, Jesus is delegating his communication to the Spirit, which implies love and trust. This is a wonderful insight into the relationships within the Trinity.

Revelation 14 also holds another superb example of Trinitarian relationships. During a time of intense persecution for the church, three angels bring messages warning about worshipping 'the beast' or 'receiving his mark', and the fate which awaits those who do[229]. John then describes that he hears a voice from heaven, presumably Jesus or the Father, saying "Write this: Blessed are the dead who die in the Lord from now on."[230] This in itself isn't unusual for Revelation, but in this instance there is a reply from the Spirit, who says "Blessed indeed, that they may rest from their labours, for their deeds follow them!"[231] These words show us that the Trinity is in agreement about what is happening. The Spirit adds detail that the first divine speaker doesn't mention. What is most pleasing is that God wanted us to be privy to this information, as the Spirit instructed John to document this occurrence.

In the closing verses of the Bible, having been shown the way in which the Spirit is so closely linked with the Father and the Son, we are shown how closely the Spirit relates to the church. In response to Jesus' declaration about himself being the root and descendent of David, we read that "The Spirit and the bride say 'come'"[232], and that

---

[229] I am making no attempt to explain who or what 'the beast', 'the mark of the beast' or 'Babylon' means in this passage; to do so is out with the scope of this book.
[230] Revelation 14:13
[231] Ibid

those who hear should echo this. The Spirit teaches us about who Jesus is, and we see the closeness that the bride shares with the Spirit, in that their response is with one voice. This, surely, should be the aim of the church; to seek ever closer fellowship with the Spirit, so that our response to Jesus becomes ever clearer.

## Conclusions

So what can we say? There is extensive biblical evidence to support the notion that the Spirit reveals information to God's people, as well as having a role in ushering along preaching and teaching. But if this is true, it requires a response from us, so as not to simply just be filed away as trivia. I would suggest three points be taken to heart. Firstly, we should recognize that wisdom, knowledge, insight and truth are products of the Spirit. As Christians, we have access to infinite wisdom, because if God truly is omniscient, He can supply us with knowledge which cannot be attained by any other path. Those Christians in business, education, in the arts or indeed in any capacity where originality and inspiration are legitimate currency are allowed and should seek the Spirit's wisdom about their field of expertise. Remember, Jesus said that the Spirit will lead us into all truth.

Secondly, I believe that the church would do well to be less sceptical when Christians encounter the Spirit. As we have seen with Peter's roof-top encounter, sometimes experiences just happen for their own sake, but sometimes these experiences are as a means to an end. Perhaps they are to shake people out of a theological rut, or else to spur them into action in a particular area. Either way, I believe that, while spiritual encounters should be weighed against Scripture, we should indeed appeal to the entirety of Scripture in the book, as opposed to the selected number of Scriptures we carry in our heads which back up our theology.

---

[232] Revelation 22:17

Finally, and following on from my previous point, Paul's comments about remarrying show us that while there are some issues about which we should not compromise, there are also some matters where it is wise to seek the counsel of the Spirit and to appeal to one's own conscience. The Spirit will not contradict Himself, because He is the Spirit of truth, and so in a situation where there is an apparent deadlock about a topic, I believe that each person in question should pray honestly, transparently seek the Spirit and humbly share this with others. I truly believe that this is a more Biblical way of moving the church forward in her mission than by appealing to democratic methods. The casting of lots occurs 23 times in the Bible; however 18 of these are in the Old Testament, four of them are in reference to the Romans dividing Jesus' clothes and only one reference of this method being used by the disciples. This one instance, in Acts 1:26, was the last thing which happened *before* we first hear about the day of Pentecost, and I believe this is intentional. The clear juxtaposition between the drawing of lots and the coming of the Spirit should point us to the impression that casting lots is an old covenant method, but something new and better has arrived. In the old covenant, only a select few people at a time had the Holy Spirit, but Pentecost makes the Spirit available to all flesh, and as such in the new covenant all of God's people can appeal to the Spirit for revelation, and He is faithful to guide.

# Six

# The Spirit Brings about God's Attributes, Covenants and Future Plans

## ✱✱✱

We have now spent a considerable amount of time exploring the role of the Spirit in revealing truth and empowering teaching. In this chapter we will look at the role of the Spirit in bringing to earth the attributes of God, as well as His covenants and plans for the future. As we shall see, the Spirit is more than just a messenger running errands for His master. Rather, the presence of the Spirit shows us what God is like and what He has promised us.

### The Old Testament

A pattern that is, no doubt, becoming apparent is that the New Testament has significantly more to say about the ministry of the Spirit than the Old Testament. The Holy Spirit is mentioned approximately three times more frequently in the New Testament, and we get substantially more information and insight into who He is and what He does from the gospels and epistles than from the Old Testament writers. The adage about the link between the New and Old Testaments is helpful here; 'The new is in the old concealed, and the old is in the new revealed.' That which appears in 'seed form' in the Old Testament should appear in 'blossom' form in the New.

This is particularly pertinent when we're discussing God's covenants and future plans, and so we must proceed with this in mind. However, it would be helpful to define what we mean by covenant before we continue. For our purposes, a covenant is a binding agreement made between God and humanity, which is still upheld if one party is unfaithful to it. In real terms, this means that God will still uphold His end of the bargain ("I will be your God") even if the people he has made the covenant with don't uphold theirs.

In Psalm 51, Jesus' ancestor, David, reflects upon his sinful actions in sleeping with Bathsheba and having her husband Uriah killed to cover it up, pleading with God to have mercy on him, to purge him of his sins and to wash him thoroughly[233]. Throughout the whole psalm you can hear David's genuine remorse, when he implores the LORD to "Cast me not away from your presence, and take not your Holy Spirit from me"[234]. The way many psalms, including this one, were written was in mirrored couplets. This means that the author would express the same idea or sentiment in two different ways, back to back. An example of this is verse 5 of this psalm;

> "Behold, I was brought forth in iniquity, and in sin did my mother conceive me."[235]

This is an ancient writing style. Notice how David expresses the idea of being 'brought forth in iniquity', and then echoes the same idea with different words; 'in sin (iniquity) did my mother conceive me (brought forth)'. So, when David writes in verse 11 for God not to cast him from His presence, and then echoes this with "and take not your Holy Spirit from me", we can be sure that David understood the presence of God to be inextricably linked with the Holy Spirit. David repeats this sentiment when, in psalm 139, he writes; "Where shall I go from your Spirit? Or where shall I flee from your presence?"[236] and concludes that there is nowhere he cannot go from His presence or His Spirit.

---

[233] Psalm 51:1-7
[234] Psalm 51:11
[235] Psalm 51:5
[236] Psalm 139:7

The Holy Spirit carries the presence of God; this is one of the attributes of God which the Spirit brings to God's people. The old covenant had prophets, priests and kings encountering the Holy Spirit, while the new covenant allows for any believer to encounter Him. Because of this, every Christian in every church has been given access to the presence of God by the Holy Spirit bought for them with Jesus' blood.

The wonderful book of Haggai describes the command given through the prophet to rebuild the temple, and the assurance that glory of the second temple would surpass that of the first. The LORD confirms to the people that the covenant He made to their fathers when they left Egypt is still standing, and that He is still with them.[237] One verse sums this up perfectly; "My Spirit remains in your midst. Fear not."[238]

Haggai is introducing us to the notion that covenant is linked with the ideas of 'presence' and 'Spirit'. God assures the people that under the covenant He made with Moses, sited here in Haggai 2, His Spirit remains in their midst, so they have nothing to fear. As we will see, God's covenants are linked with God's presence by His Spirit, and this thread weaves its way through Scripture and culminates in the Spirit being poured out at Pentecost.

However, before we discuss Pentecost, there are a number of other references to the link between 'presence' and 'covenant' in the Old Testament. Isaiah writes that God will "pour water on thirsty land",[239] meaning that He will pour His Spirit on their offspring, and His blessing on their descendants[240]. Notice again the link between 'the Spirit' and 'the blessing poured on descendants'. Isaiah mentions this link again later on, when he writes;

---

[237] Haggai 2:1-5
[238] Haggai 2:5
[239] Isaiah 44:3
[240] Ibid.

> "And as for me, this is my covenant with them," says the
> LORD: "My Spirit that is upon you, and my words that I have
> put in your mouth, shall not depart out of your mouth, or
> out of the mouth of your offspring..."[241]

Isaiah is writing of the redemption that will come to God's people through the Messiah, but notice that the concept of covenant is again accompanied with promises that the Spirit will remain with them. The often eccentric prophet Ezekiel also writes about the Spirit being poured out on God's people when describing their return from exile and a vision of the new temple[242]. A few chapters after this, Ezekiel goes on to describe the glory of the LORD coming to fill that new temple. He describes it as "like the sound of many waters"[243], which is a phrase ascribed to Jesus' voice in Revelation 1. Ezekiel falls on his face, but the Spirit brings him into the inner court, and the glory of God fills the temple[244].

While we should use caution in definitively saying that a certain prophetic passage means this or that, it seems that in this instance the Spirit was instrumental in ushering the prophet into the presence of God. The link to Revelation 1 indicates that perhaps Ezekiel was seeing an eschatological vision of Christ. If this is the case, we can line this passage up with the belief that the Spirit is instrumental in bringing people into the presence of God in our day as well as several millennia ago. However, as I've said, caution should be used when making absolute statements about such passages, but the least we can observe is another link between the work of the Spirit and God's glory and presence.

---

[241] Isaiah 59:21
[242] Ezekiel 39:29
[243] Ezekiel 43:2
[244] Ezekiel 43:3-5

## Covenant in the New Testament

The New Testament sheds more light on the relationship between the Spirit and bringing God's covenants. The first hint of a shift between the former old covenant with Israel and the present covenant with all people is found in Matthew 12, where Matthew comments on Jesus' healing ministry by referring to Isaiah 61, where God says "I will put my Spirit upon him, and he will proclaim justice to the Gentiles"[245]. Up until the time of Jesus, covenants were between God and His people. Individual gentiles could join God's people and thus benefit from the covenant, Ruth for example, but in general most covenants weren't extended to gentiles. That is, until Jesus. Matthew connects the prophesy in Isaiah with the ministry of Jesus which he saw before his eyes; that His purpose was to redeem the whole world, not just the Jews.

Paul makes an interesting observation about the role of the Spirit in covenants in Romans 7, when he talks about being released from the law through the death of Christ. He makes the distinction between the "old way of the written code"[246] which held us captive, with our ability to "serve in the new way of the Spirit"[247]. Paul purposefully contrasts the 'old written code', or some translations render this phrase as 'the old way of the letter', with the 'new way of the Spirit'. We know from the very next verse that he is talking about the law, the Mosaic covenant, and so Paul is saying that the present covenant, by which Christian believers can know God, is 'of the Spirit'.

Paul spends a lot of time in Romans 8 talking about what living in the covenant of the Spirit actually looks like, that being to live 'according to the Spirit' which is to set one's mind on the things of the Spirit[248]. This echoes what he writes to the Galatian church, that

---

[245] Matthew 12:18
[246] Romans 7:6
[247] Ibid.
[248] Romans 8:5

where you sow, either to the flesh or to the Spirit, is where you will reap[249]. However, the produce of these different 'masters' are as different as they are; the flesh yields corruption, whereas the Spirit yields eternal life. What Paul is saying here is that where you invest your time, energy and ultimately your life is the same place from which you will draw.

In these passages, Paul is explaining that our glorious inheritance won by Christ is stunted if we fail to live in the good of it. Living according to the Spirit enables the believer in Jesus to overcome the desires of the flesh; literally this means that the believer is able to say no. The German philosopher Immanuel Kant, in his book 'the critique of pure reason', said that being 'free' to fulfil our desires is not freedom; we are really slaves to those desires. Freedom is the opposite of necessity[250]. For the Christian, Jesus has secured that freedom and the ability to say no to the desires of the flesh which, as the writer to the Hebrews puts it, "so easily entangles"[251]. We will discuss Romans 8 later in this chapter, but for now we can be assured that it is the Spirit who has brought about this covenant which has united us with our Father and given us freedom.

Paul adds to this thought in 2 Corinthians 3, where he explains that God has made us sufficient to be "ministers of a new covenant, not of the letter but of the Spirit"[252]. This is a very interesting passage, as it was written to the whole church that is in Corinth, not just to the leaders of that church[253]. Paul is affirming that all of the people in the church, and not just a select few, may minister this covenant to other people. This is in contrast with the old covenant of the letter, where only an elite group would be allowed or able to teach from the Torah. Paul echoes his sentiment from Romans 7 by saying that 'the letter kills, but the Spirit gives life.' Because this new

---

[249] Galatians 6:8
[250] Michael Sandel, *'Justice'*, London: Penguin, 2010, p108
[251] Hebrews 12:1
[252] 2 Corinthians 3:6
[253] 2 Corinthians 1:1

covenant is of the Spirit and not of the letter, every believer can impart Christ to someone else, because every believer has the Spirit living inside them. Both Paul and Jesus were at pains to stress that the law in itself was not bad, wrong or sinful, but rather that it in itself does not lead to life. The law points to something; the need for a saviour. This saviour brings a new covenant, a new way of doing things, which says that anyone, male or female, slave or free, Jew or Greek may be a minister of His grace to the needy world.

## The Spirit as a Guarantee in the New Testament

While it might seem counterintuitive to promise someone something they already possess, this is the situation we find in the New Testament concerning what God has in store for believers. We are told that every believer in Christ has the Spirit living inside them, that individually and collectively these believers form the temple of the Holy Spirit, and that, as we have just seen, the Spirit paves the way to eternal life by bringing God's covenantal promises. In addition to all these things being true, the promises we find in Paul's letters set out a series of future events which are promised to us by the Spirit.

The first of these we find in Romans 8, where Paul describes our current possession of the Spirit as being "the firstfruits"[254]. Unsurprisingly, this word 'firstfruits' has agricultural roots, as it was used to describe the portion of the harvest which would be offered to God, or the first part of the dough from which sacred loaves would be prepared. In this context, Paul is using this word to describe the initial product of a person's conversion, but gathering a 'firstfruit' implies that there is a fuller harvest still to be gathered. The natural question to ask in light of this is 'what is the full harvest?' The answer is found in these verses in Romans 8, and has several aspects.

---

[254] Romans 8:23

Firstly, "we ourselves … wait eagerly for adoption as sons, the redemption of our bodies"[255]. Paul is expressing that we are awaiting our adoption as sons of God. There is an element of 'now and not yet' about this statement, because, as we will see later in this chapter, Scripture tells us that we are presently sons of God. However, it seems that our being adopted as sons of God is a firstfruit, and that a fuller realisation of this awaits us in the next life. The second aspect of the fuller harvest is found in verse 25, where Paul says that we wait for what is unseen, and we do so patiently[256]. That which is presently unseen is the fullness of the kingdom of heaven; God's sovereign rule over all the earth.

Paul makes several more references to the Spirit as a guarantee, or a promise, of something yet better. It is easy to understand the difficulty the early church would have had in shifting their mind-set from the covenant written by Moses to the covenant written in Jesus' blood. In a similar way, we who have never known anything other than the new covenant may have trouble imagining something better than what we already have. What these verses show us is that there is something better, and it is promised to us. In 2 Corinthians, Paul speaks of God establishing himself, Silas and Timothy with the Corinthian church in Christ, anointing them, and also giving them His Spirit in their hearts as a guarantee[257]. Later in this letter, Paul talks about the heavenly dwelling prepared for believers, for which the Spirit is a guarantee[258]. The Greek word translated as 'guarantee' in these two passages, '*arrabone*', originates in financial terminology, literally meaning a sum of money given as a promise that the full amount will be paid in the future. We might translate this word as 'down payment' or 'deposit'. The message given in 2 Corinthians is that being given the Spirit is a blessing in itself, but the Spirit is also

---

[255] Ibid.
[256] Romans 8:25
[257] 2 Corinthians 1:21-22
[258] 2 Corinthians 5:5

a promise of future blessings, in greater measures than we currently know.

We also find this word used in Ephesians 1, where Paul again writes of the inheritance which has been secured for those who heard the word of truth, and who believed in Jesus, and were sealed with "the promised Holy Spirit, who is the guarantee of our inheritance until we acquire possession of it"[259]. Here, the Spirit is described as being something that was promised[260], but also as the promise of something else; our heavenly inheritance. In Ephesians 4 we find similar language, when Paul instructs the Ephesians not to grieve the Holy Spirit of God, "by whom you were sealed for the day of redemption"[261]. The idea of something being sealed conjures the imagery of sending a letter, where the writer would imprint his initials into the wax which sealed the letter closed. This metaphor is telling us that we bear the imprint of our author, Christ[262], but also that there is more to come, because the Spirit living within us is the deposit which guarantees the full payment.

Along slightly different lines, we find Paul instructing Timothy in the second letter bearing his name to stay faithful to his mission, to not be ashamed of what he believes and to follow the pattern Paul has set out for him. He exhorts him to, "By the Holy Spirit who dwells within us, guard the good deposit entrusted to you"[263]. The 'good deposit' entrusted to Timothy is, verse 13 of chapter 1 tells us, the faith and love that are in Christ Jesus, given to Timothy to steward. The phrasing of these verses does make one think that Timothy is being told to guard this good deposit by the power given through the Holy Spirit. Thinking of this in the context of what Paul wrote to the Ephesians and to the Corinthians, it makes sense to appeal to the Spirit to guard the Gospel in our hearts.

---

[259] Ephesians 1:13-14
[260] See Galatians 3:24 – 4:7
[261] Ephesians 4:30
[262] Hebrews 12:2, NKJV
[263] 2 Timothy 1:14

## The Spirit brings Joy

A common perception of the church held by those who do not attend regularly is that it's boring. In some instances, depending on personal preference, this might be correct. Many people may think of church as being a place of solemnity, repentance, guilt and shame. Interestingly, while there is certainly a place for solemnity and repentance, we find nothing in the Bible about God seeking to bring guilt and shame on His people. Rather, we find countless references in the Old Testament to God being the one who acquits the guilty and who provides a sacrificial system by which people could expunge their guilt. In the New Testament, guilt is mentioned only 15 times, and it is never ascribed to people who belong to God. Of course, those who sin are guilty of committing sin, but part of Christ's mission is to "sustain you to the end, guiltless in the day of our Lord Jesus Christ"[264]. Jesus came to take our guilt and shame, not to add to our guilt and shame. This is what the reformer Martin Luther called 'the great exchange'; we get all of Jesus' righteousness and He got all of our sin, guilt and shame[265]. Upon the dedication of the temple, David, even as a man of the old covenant, remarked that God had turned his mourning into dancing[266]. How much more so can we of the new covenant say that? And so we naturally turn to explore the Spirit bringing joy to God's people.

In Luke 10, we find Jesus sending out the seventy-two to heal the sick and proclaim the kingdom of God, and then 'rejoicing in the Holy Spirit' upon their return[267]. The word translated as 'rejoice' means to exult and be exceedingly glad. It seems that Jesus was so thrilled when they reported that demons were subject to them in His name, that his response was to rejoice in the Holy Spirit. After all, the instructions He gave to the seventy-two have some resonance to the

---

[264] 1 Corinthians 1:8
[265] D. K. McKim, 'The Cambridge Companion to Martin Luther', Cambridge: Cambridge Univeristy Press, 2003, p145
[266] Psalm 30:11
[267] Luke 10:21

instructions given to the church before He ascended; maybe Jesus had seen His church in a miniature form and was rejoicing because those who he sent had understood their mission and had seen some fruit. This is the first time such a phrase is found in the New Testament, and it would be difficult to understand, if we were to look at it in isolation.

In the book of Acts, we read of Paul and Barnabas with the Antioch church and of their being persecuted by the Jewish leaders, resulting in Paul and Barnabas being driven from the region to Iconium[268]. Acts 13:52 tells us the response to this event is that "the disciples were filled with joy and with the Holy Spirit." It's not clear from the passage which disciples were filled with the Holy Spirit, whether those in Antioch, those in Iconium or those who travelled with Paul and Barnabas. However, this is beside the point; the response to this situation was that *some* disciples were filled with joy and with the Holy Spirit. We will explore what it means to be filled with the Holy Spirit in chapter 8, but what does it mean to be 'filled with joy'?

Joy literally means 'gladness', and is found more than 50 times in the New Testament. So, in essence, to be filled with joy is to abound with gladness, to be ridiculously happy in spite of circumstances. Joy is listed in Galatians 5 as one of the fruit of the Spirit[269]. The context of Galatians 5 shows us that the fruit of the Spirit is not talking about apples and oranges, but rather 'fruit' as being the effect or result of something. Ergo, we could read Galatians 5:22 as, 'but the result of the Spirit is love, joy, peace...' We should also notice that joy is listed as separate from peace, rightly so as they're different words in the Greek. While 'joy' is to abound with gladness, 'peace' means for the soul to rest in a tranquil state, assured of its salvation[270]. They do indeed share a source, that being the Spirit, but they are different products. Just as the same rain can fall on different fields and

---

Acts 13:50-51
[269] Galatians 5:22
[270]http://www.blueletterbible.org/lang/lexicon/lexicon.cfm?Strongs=G151
5andt=KJV, retrieved 8/2/2013

produce both strawberries and wheat, so too the same Spirit brings forth different results. However, these different outcomes should occur in the same person, because in Galatians 5 Paul does not write about the 'fruits' of the Spirit, implying a plural from which we can choose, but rather the 'fruit' of the Spirit, which cannot be subdivided. Of the 66 Biblical uses of the word translated as 'fruit', 12 of them are rendered using the plural 'fruits'. Galatians 5 is not one of those 12 verses, so we can conclude that joy and peace are different expressions of one product. Where one abounds, the other should be nearby.

It may seem obvious that these two concepts are distinct, and yet many Christians blur the two, often without meaning to. We must ask ourselves if a religious spirit has crept into our churches and into our hearts if we treat someone demonstrating extreme happiness (joy) with more suspicion than someone demonstrating extreme serenity (peace). If suspicion or resentment is our response to this, I believe that it says more about our own hearts than those of the person demonstrating joy or peace, or for that matter any of the fruit of the Spirit. On average, children laugh 150 times a day, while adults laugh about 6 times a day[271]; Jesus told us to be more like children[272]. We must ask in such situations; what is the end product of the encounter that someone is having? Are they closer to God, more Christ-like? Or are they more conceited and boastful in themselves and in their own achievements? As Jesus said, "each tree is known by its own fruit"[273].

Paul mentions the joy of the Holy Spirit twice more in his letters, in Romans 14 and 1 Thessalonians 1. In 1 Thessalonians, Paul commends the church for becoming imitators of himself and his fellow workers, and for receiving the word among much affliction,

---

[271] N. Gumble,
https://twitter.com/nickygumbel/status/299640361746309120, retrieved 8/2/2013
[272] Matthew 18:3
[273] Luke 6:44

"with the joy of the Holy Spirit"[274]. In this instance, the joy of the Holy Spirit is a product of His ministry with particular emphasis on overcoming adverse circumstances. Romans 14 paints a similar picture as that which we find in Galatians 5 and Acts 13, where Paul distinguishes joy from peace, but also adds righteousness into the equation. The context of this passage is to not cause a brother to stumble by using the freedom found in Christ to eat and drink whatever we wish, but rather to abstain from, for example, eating meat or drinking alcohol if doing so would "destroy those for whom Christ died"[275]. Paul explains that the matters of eating and drinking are not the main issue in kingdom of God, as they were under the old covenant, but instead we are to pursue righteousness, peace and joy in the Holy Spirit.

Are we to construe from this passage that the Holy Spirit is the bringer of joy only, or that the Holy Spirit is the bringer of righteousness, peace and joy? Given what we've read in Galatians 5 where both joy and peace are listed as fruit of the Spirit, I believe that it's safe to read this passage as the Spirit brings peace and righteousness as well as joy. Should we not seek to experience the joy of the Lord? Should we not seek the Spirit who brings forth joy, even when our circumstances dictate that we should despair? The faith that we have in Jesus says things are okay, even when they're not okay. That is, temporally our world might be falling apart; eternally we are safe in the arms of our Father.

### The Spirit tells us that we are children of God

Throughout the New Testament we find a recurring theme appearing, which explains that while we used to be alienated from God, we have now been brought near to him, and not only that, but we have actually been adopted by Him. God whom we formerly saw as Judge has become God whom we can call 'Father'. This is a significant shift in the relationship between God and humanity,

---

274 1 Thessalonians 1:6
275 Romans 14:15-17

because whereas in the Old Testament God could be called 'Father' in a corporate way as part of the nation of Israel, Jesus' sacrifice on the cross not only 'settled the score' so we can avoid wrath, but also 'credited our account' so we can boldly approach a Holy God. There are several books on the subject of God as our Father[276], and while we don't have time to do this astounding doctrine justice, we can focus instead on the role of the Spirit in helping us to understand this truth.

It is in Paul's epistles that we are told about Christians being children of God, and that the Spirit makes this so. We come first to Romans 8, where even the opening line tells us that there is "now no condemnation for those who are in Christ Jesus"[277]. Notice the use of the word 'now', which implies that while this is presently the case, it wasn't always so. There is no blame, disapproval or attack coming our way because if we are *in* Christ, we receive everything He deserves. The old has gone, the new has come. Paul continues from verse 14, saying;

> "...all who are led by the Spirit of God are sons of God. For you did not receive the spirit of slavery to fall back into fear, but you have received the Spirit of adoption as sons, by whom we cry, "Abba! Father!" The Spirit himself bears witness with our spirit that we are children of God, and if children, then heirs—heirs of God and fellow heirs with Christ, provided we suffer with him in order that we may also be glorified with him"[278].

Scores of volumes could be written about these four verses alone because they say so much. In my opinion, these verses are as good a summary of the Christian faith as John 3:16. Beginning with verse

---

[276] Including, 'I am your Father' by Mark Stibbe, 'Experiencing Father's Embrace' by Jack Frost, 'The Father Heart of God' by Floyd McClung and 'I dared call Him Father' by Bilquis Sheikh.
[277] Romans 8:1
[278] Romans 8:14-17

14, Paul tells us that those who are led by the Spirit of God are sons of God. This begs the question, 'who is led by the Spirit of God?' Anyone who calls themselves a Christian is, whether they know it or not, being led by the Spirit. We know this from 1 Corinthians 12, where Paul explains that no one can say "Jesus is Lord except by the Spirit"[279]. Surely, saying 'Jesus is Lord' is the very essence of what it is to be a Christian?

So, we can say that all Christians are led by the Spirit of God, and so all Christians are sons of God. Of course, we are not sons of God on our own merit, but rather we inherit as a free gift what Jesus has earned at such a cost. The Spirit that leads us into the truth of these matters is referred to in verse 15 as 'the Spirit of adoption'; it is one of His roles to assure us that this is true. Paul is at pains to emphasise that we did not receive a spirit of slavery to fall back into fear. He makes this point starkly because these two 'states of being' are incompatible with one another. You cannot be a slave and a son at the same time. Jesus spoke about the same issue in John 8, where he tells the Jews who are conversing with Him that "everyone who practices sin is a slave to sin"[280]. Jesus goes on to explain that slaves are not permanent members of the household, whereas sons remain in the house forever, and if the Son sets you free, you are free indeed[281]. A son is greater than a slave.

A slave-master will command his slaves to be a certain way, he will treat them as his property to be bought and sold, to be used as he sees fit. The slave has no rights, and is treated as a commodity. Those who sin are slaves to sin. However, a father will train his son to wield freedom rightly. A father offers trust to his son, having faith that that this trust won't be abused. The father loves his son and is jealous for his wellbeing. The son has all the rights of the father, the right to his affection, his ear and his inheritance. Slaves and sons are

---

[279] 1 Corinthians 12:3
[280] John 8:34
[281] John 8:35-36

polar opposites, because they answer to a different master. Sons of God answer to God, slaves of sin answer to the father of lies[282].

The Spirit not only adopts us as sons, but He causes us to *feel* like we are adopted as sons. In addition to the Spirit preventing us from falling back into fear of slavery, He causes us to cry out to God in a personal way; "Abba, Father!"[283] As we have discussed in chapter 5, this word 'Abba' is a personal term for a Father, but even the word 'Father' is a radical expression to use for Almighty God. The combination of 'Abba' with 'Father' is an invitation to address the creator and sustained of the universe as 'Dad'. Not only are we *invited* to become sons of God, as if someone could be a Christian without being a son, but John tells us in the opening chapter of his gospel that we have been given the *right* to become children of God.[284] This is a part of our inheritance what we get from believing in Christ.

Paul describes us as fellow heirs with Christ, meaning that we get to inherit all the benefits that are due to Jesus. Paul does clarify this statement, saying that this path to glory may well be strewn with sufferings, but that at the end of this we're glorified with Christ. Being a fellow-heir means being invited to share in the reward that Jesus earned, which is an altogether mighty privilege.

Some may question my use of the word 'sons' to make reference to all Christians. Surely, female Christians are to be called 'daughters'? There are two responses to this sentiment. Firstly, the Greek word used in Romans 8 and Galatians 4 is *'huios'*, which can be either translated as 'male offspring', or else as 'those who revere God as their Father', depending on the context. I am simply using the word Paul used in these letters. Secondly, women are certainly not excluded from this inheritance, as we find in John 1 that we have been given the "right to become children of God"[285]. The word

---

[282] John 8:33, John 8:44
[283] Romans 8:15, Galatians 4:6
[284] John 1:12
[285] John 1:12

'children' translated from the word *'teknon'* and can refer to both male and female offspring. There is a specific word for daughter, *'thygater'*, which is used on one occasion to refer to God becoming our Father in 2 Corinthians 6, where Paul writes;

> "...then I will welcome you, and I will be a father to you, and you shall be sons and daughters to me, says the Lord Almighty"[286].

This positively affirms that both men and women are children of God. My second reason for using 'sons' is because the context into which these letters were written was one where, in natural family relations, a family with one son and one daughter would see the son inherit everything, whereas the daughter would inherit nothing. I believe Paul used 'sons' to make a point to the Roman and Galatian churches (which would have mostly consisted of women, slaves and the poor) that in Christ their inheritance is not based on their gender, occupation or income, but rather on Jesus. Paul calls his Christian recipients 'sons' to affirm that they will all inherit what Christ has won for them.

In light of these amazing truths about who our heavenly Father has made us to be, I believe we should carefully consider some of the songs we hold so dear in church. 'Amazing Grace', for example, by John Newton speaks about the ridiculous love poured out on people, but in the same breath makes reference to the singer being 'a wretch'. Now, in fairness to this song, it does distinguish between the past and the present states of the soul ('I once was lost, but now am found'), but if a song we are singing leads us to sing or believe that a Christian is a slave as opposed to a son, it should be avoided. This is because if we are in Christ, we are saints, not sinners. We might sin, but our identity remains as sons. We cannot be in Christ *and* in our sin, and so our worship should not imply that we are.

---

[286] 2 Corinthians 6:17-18

## The Spirit brings comfort

Being declared as a son of almighty God is a cause of endless thanksgiving. We are safe in the arms of the Lord of the universe, and loved by Him unconditionally; that is, God loves you as much as He loves Jesus. This truth should be a great comfort in times of trial, but there are several references to the Spirit bringing specific comfort to God's people. Jesus refers to the Holy Spirit as a 'helper' in the gospel of John[287]. Another example of this is found in Acts 9, where we read that the church in Judea, Galilee and Samaria had peace and was being built up, and that it multiplied by "walking in the fear of the Lord and the comfort of the Holy Spirit"[288]. This is an interesting phrase, as it tells of a tension that the church as a whole felt; that being between the fear of the Lord and the comfort of the Holy Spirit. Remarkably, the Spirit which brought comfort was the same Lord whom the disciples feared. Reading the whole of Acts leads us to determine that the fear they felt was a reverent fear, as opposed to a threatening fear. It seems that while the church held a reverent fear of the Lord, the Spirit brought comfort with this. In chapter 9 we will discuss the deity of the Holy Spirit, but here we find the Sprit bringing comfort to the church in light of the conversion of Saul and the fallout this brought.

Many years after his conversion, Paul-who-was-Saul is writing to the church he founded in Philippi, and assures them that though he is imprisoned, through the prayers of the Philippian church and "the help of the Spirit of Jesus Christ", he will find his deliverance[289]. Paul is relying on the prayers of his friends and on the Spirit (of Christ) to give him strength in a very serious situation. Peter writes along similar lines in his first letter, saying that when you are insulted for the name of Christ, you are blessed, because the Spirit of glory and of God rests upon you[290]. Often in the UK, which has been held as a

---

[287] John 14:26, 15:26, 16:7
[288] Acts 9:31
[289] Philippians
[290] 1 Peter 4:14

'Christian country' for so long by so many, we can forget this verse and instead appeal to the law of religious liberty in times of distress. However, the fact is that all Christians will receive troubles, but we should not fear this, as Jesus has overcome the world[291]. A healthy perspective is, when we receive insults or abuse because of our Christian convictions, to count this as a blessing because Jesus was also insulted; we are following in his footsteps. In fact, Jesus says elsewhere that it is when all people speak well of us that we should be wary[292]. But Peter tells us that the Spirit of glory and of God rests upon us.

### The Spirit brings God's presence

There is a lot to say about the presence of God, and other authors have already trodden this path[293]. For our purposes, we will explore the role the Spirit plays in bringing God's presence to his people. Of course, the believer and the gathered church is the temple of the Holy Spirit, where God dwells, and we will explore this more in chapter 8. However, there are a few other references to the Spirit bringing God's presence to God's people, such as we find in 2 Corinthians 3, where Paul writes that "...the Lord is the Spirit, and where the Spirit of the Lord is, there is freedom"[294]. This verse affirms that where the Spirit of the Lord dwells, freedom comes as a result. A natural question to ask in response to this is, 'freedom from what?' The proceeding verses give the answer; freedom from the constraints of the old covenant. Paul is writing here about the veil that Moses placed over his face after ascending Mount Sinai to be given the Law. Paul then compares this to what we have in Christ, when "we all, with unveiled face, [behold] the glory of the Lord"[295].

---

[291] John 16:33
[292] Luke 626
[293] A substantial example of this is 'The practice of the presence of God; the best rule of a holy life' by Brother Lawrence, available for free online.
[294] 2 Corinthians 3:17
[295] 2 Corinthians 3:18

We behold the Lord's glory in His presence, and by the Spirit we are free and able to do this.

Two other references are made to the Spirit with reference to the presence of God, both of which are found in the book of Revelation. John uses the phrase "I was in the Spirit" on two occasions; firstly in Revelation 1 as he is introducing his book. John goes on to explain that while 'in the Spirit', he heard a voice telling him to write down what he would see and to send it to seven churches[296]. The voice he hears turns out to be that of Jesus, glorified and radiant. John is in the presence of the risen Lord, the one true God as a result of being 'in the Spirit'. Notice that he was 'in the Spirit' before Jesus addressed him, and the way that it is written gives the impression that this wasn't a one-off event, but rather something he did regularly. After all, John was an old man when these events happened to him, and had been exiled to the rocky island of Patmos alone; it makes sense that this follower of Jesus would spend time in the Spirit.

The other reference to being 'in the Spirit' is found in Revelation 4. The passage deserves to be read in full;

> "After this I looked, and behold, a door standing open in heaven! And the first voice, which I had heard speaking to me like a trumpet, said, "Come up here, and I will show you what must take place after this." At once I was in the Spirit, and behold, a throne stood in heaven, with one seated on the throne"[297].

Notice that this voice which John hears in Revelation 4 is the same voice which he heard in Revelation 1; Jesus Christ, his friend and his God. John once again is 'in the Spirit' and sees heaven and a vision of what must happen after, meaning in the future. Revelation is divided into two parts; the present for John in Revelation 1 to 3, and

---

[296] Revelation 1:10
[297] Revelation 4:1-2

the future for John and us from Revelation 4. Again, he is 'in the Spirit' when these things take place, but unlike in Revelation 1, he sees the vision *before* he is 'in the Spirit'. The catalyst for both examples is being 'in the Spirit', but being in the Spirit brings the person into the presence of God in a profound way.

**The Spirit brings love**

As will be becoming apparent, with each of these attributes brought about by the Spirit there is a significant link to the Spirit being fully God. This is to be expected, because we cannot separate the deity of the Spirit from the divine attributes which He brings about. Where the Spirit is, God fully is. So finally we explore the Spirit bringing the love of God to us. Many of us will be familiar with the verse in 1 John which tells us that God is love[298]. But the role of the Spirit in applying God's love to us is less familiar. To discover this, we must turn again to the writings of the apostle Paul.

In Romans 5, Paul is writing that through sufferings we might find endurance, and endurance leads to character which gives us hope, and hope does not put us to shame[299]. He then justifies this by saying that God's love has been poured into our hearts by the Holy Spirit[300]. We are loved by God, and God's love is applied to our lives by the Spirit. Paul refers to this again ten chapters later, when appealing to the Roman church to pray for him that he might be released and able to visit them. He urges them to pray for him 'by the love of the Spirit'; that is, by the love poured into their hearts by the Spirit. Out of the depth of relationship the church had with Paul, he asks for their prayers.

When writing to the Corinthian church, Paul lists how he and his companions overcame the various trials that they faced. He describes how he overcame a myriad of trials "by purity, knowledge,

---

[298] 1 John 4:8
[299] Romans 5:3-5
[300] Romans 5:5

patience, kindness, the Holy Spirit, genuine love"[301]. Unlike the two passages in Romans, Paul doesn't specify that the genuine love he experienced was *of* the Holy Spirit, but rather he puts 'the Holy Spirit' and 'genuine love' immediately next to each other, which seems to suggest a connection. If we read this passage while keeping Galatians 5 in mind, we see several of the fruit of the Spirit listed in this verse; patience, kindness and love, which are products of the Spirit. We read a similar list in Philippians 2 when Paul, appealing to the Philippians to be of one mind, asks "So if there is any encouragement in Christ, any comfort from love, any participation in the Spirit, any affection and sympathy"[302]. Notice again that the mentions of 'love' and 'the Spirit' are placed next to each other. I believe that this is because where the Spirit is, the result is an atmosphere of love. If love is a result (fruit) of the Spirit, we should expect the atmosphere where the Spirit is present to be a loving one. Conversely, people who boast in the Spirit but are not loving should be scrutinized before absolute trust is placed in them.

### Conclusions

Having now examined how the Spirit brings God's attributes and covenants into our lives, we can conclude with several truths. Firstly, we have seen from both the Old and New Testaments that where the Spirit is, God's presence is. Now, if every believer has the Spirit living inside them, it stands to reason that every believer can experience the presence of God the Spirit in a meaningful way.

Secondly, if it is true that every believer is, as Paul says in 2 Corinthians 3, a 'minister of the new covenant', is it not time to re-evaluate the divide between so-called 'clergy' and so-called 'laity' in certain denominations? Of course, there is a place for gifted people to have a leadership role, and I am not advocating a free-for all. But an emphasis should be placed on empowering and equipping the

---

[301] 2 Corinthians 6:6
[302] Philippians 2:1

whole church to minister the new covenant to the world, instead of leaving it to 'the minister', 'the evangelist' or simply 'someone else'.

Thirdly, the Spirit is Himself an inheritance, but this inheritance also functions as a down-payment for something greater. In light of this, we can, and should, seek more of God each day. By this I don't mean more theology or more understanding, as useful and necessary as these disciplines are; if we believe that God can be known personally, we need to seek Him personally. But because God is infinite, we can eternally seek to know Him more. If we have decided to settle for what we already have of, and know about, God, this is what we'll get. However, there is always more to seek and learn and experience.

Finally, I believe that the church as a whole needs to grasp more fully what Paul writes about in Romans 8, that there is a profound difference between being a slave and being a son. I believe that there is an element of nominative determinism at work in this regard; you become what you believe you are. If you believe that you are a sinner who is bound to sin, you might spend your whole life either sinning in secret or else putting up rules to keep you from sin, but in your heart you haven't died to it. However, if you believe that you are a beloved child of God, who at immeasurable price to Himself secured your forgiveness with the blood of His Son, who seeks your good and desires to love and know you more, who loves you based not on what you do but based on what Jesus has done for you, the result will be one of profound gratitude and affection. In other words, if you focus on avoiding sin, you're looking at the wrong object, because you're still looking at sin. If you focus on Jesus, though you may stumble, you will find sin dead to you already. Yet we needn't do it out of our own strength; the Spirit is ready and willing to make us believe and feel like we're sons of God.

# Seven

# The Spirit Leads, Instructs and Compels

### ✳✳✳

I wonder how many people have had similar conversations to those I have from time to time, which include phrases like "the Spirit told me to do that" or "I felt led by the Spirit to tell you this..."? I often don't know how to take these statements, and I don't think I'm the only one who feels this way. I am very sure that one reason for this is because, for a long time, I could not honestly say that I had had similar experiences. But this does beg the question as to whether these sentiments have any basis in Scripture, and if so, how should we respond when on the receiving end? Does the Spirit indeed instruct, lead and compel people to do or say certain things?

## The Old Testament

In the first book of Kings, the prophet Obadiah is looking for water and grass for King Ahab's livestock, and while doing so meets the prophet Elijah on the road. When Elijah asks Obadiah to go and tell Ahab that he is in the region, this causes Obadiah some distress[303]. He fears that Ahab will seek to kill him, despite having "feared the LORD from his youth"[304]. Obadiah fears for his life is because he believes that as soon as he has finished speaking with him, Elijah will be carried away by the Spirit of the LORD to an unknown location[305]. He fears that when Ahab doesn't find Elijah that he will meet the same gruesome fate as the prophets did at the hands of Jezebel[306].

---

[303] 1 Kings 18:7-14
[304] 1 Kings 18:12
[305] 1 Kings 18:12

However, this worry doesn't go unheeded, and so Elijah agrees to meet Ahab.

Curiously, Elijah doesn't correct Obadiah's belief that the Spirit will carry him away. This could just be a turn of phrase meaning that the mantle of being a prophet will take him away along other paths before Ahab arrives. However, this could mean that the Spirit will lift him up and physically take him to another location, quite apart from the normal methods of walking or riding. The Hebrew word in question, 'nasa', seems to lend itself to this second interpretation, as in its other usage throughout the Old Testament it is used to mean 'lift up' or 'carry', as opposed to 'usher' or 'compel'. Nor is this the only occurrence of the Spirit doing something like this, as we shall see throughout this chapter.

We see this phrase again in the second book of Kings, just after Elisha sees Elijah taken up to heaven in a whirlwind, the sons of the prophets of Jericho 'transfer' their loyalty to Elisha. However, the sons of the prophets don't fully appreciate what has happened, and ask for permission to go and look for Elijah[307]. They believe that he is very much alive, but that "It may be that the Spirit of the LORD has caught him up and cast him upon some mountain or into some valley"[308]. Reading these verses in isolation, this might sound like a strange conclusion, but given what we have just considered in 1 Kings 18, Elijah's followers are clearly assuming that he has been physically moved by the Spirit once again. They have already pledged their allegiance to Elisha, but they refer to Elijah as 'your master'[309] when speaking to Elisha, so it seems that while they recognise that a transfer of power has taken place, they want to make sure that Elijah is alright. Notice here that, again, no one in this instance assumes that being 'caught up' by the Spirit is a ridiculous idea.

---

[306] 1 Kings 18:13-14
[307] 2 Kings 2:15-16
[308] 2 Kings 2:16
[309] 2 Kings 2:16

Ezekiel has a lot to say about this type of happening. He tells us that as he was being commissioned to be sent to the nation of Israel, that the Spirit 'lifted him up', and he heard 'the voice of a great earthquake' saying to him, "blessed be the glory of the LORD from its place"[310]. This 'voice' turns out to be the noise of the wings of the living creatures, and of the heavenly wheels turning, which are described in Ezekiel 1. Just reading the writings of this prophet should lift our eyes to the fact that sometimes things which appear 'weird' to us are simply what heaven looks like. While we should not accept something on the sole basis that it's weird, we shouldn't dismiss weird phenomena out of hand either, as these may be the heartbeat of our heavenly home.

We see the phrase "the Spirit lifted me up" just a few verses later, where Ezekiel describes the Spirit taking him away because the hand of the LORD was strong upon him, and he is deposited with the exiles at Tel-abib[311]. In both of these instances, the Spirit seems to literally lift Ezekiel up, in the former to see a heavenly vision, the latter to take him to a different geographical location. These are challenging verses, for if someone were to come into one of our churches and declare that the Spirit had physically brought him there, and on the way he had been shown a heavenly vision, how would we react? Do our expectations match up with the revelation of Scripture, or have we domesticated the Spirit to keep ourselves comfortable? There is, of course, a difference between an Old Testament prophet and a New Testament believer, but these occurrences are not confined to the Old Testament, as we shall see later in this chapter.

Ezekiel has many similar experiences, nine in all, over the course of his book. Later in chapter 3, Ezekiel is led by the LORD into a valley, and the glory of the LORD appears before him. His understandable response is to fall on his face, but the Spirit 'entered into him and

---

[310] Ezekiel 3:12
[311] Ezekiel 3:14-15

stood him on his feet', before giving him further instructions[312]. Again here we see the Spirit physically moving Ezekiel. In chapter 8, the Spirit again lifts Ezekiel up between heaven and earth and brings him 'in visions of God to Jerusalem' to witness the abomination of the temple there[313]. Whether Ezekiel was, in this instance, physically taken to Jerusalem, or else just shown a vision of Jerusalem is beside the point; either way, the Spirit was compelling him along. In chapter 11 Ezekiel is again 'lifted up by the Spirit' and brought to the eastern gate of the temple, where he is told to prophesy against the wicked counsellors of the city[314]. Later in this chapter Ezekiel has another visionary encounter, where he is lifted up by the Spirit and brought to the exiles in Chaldea to tell them what the LORD had shown him[315]. Then, in chapter 37, we find one of the most well-known passages from Ezekiel; the valley of dry bones. Ezekiel is brought to the valley 'in the Spirit of the LORD', and commanded to prophesy over the bones until they live[316]. The final instance in the Old Testament of the Spirit 'lifting someone up' and bringing them to a certain place is in Ezekiel 43:5, where Ezekiel is lifted up by the Spirit and brought into the inner court of the temple, and the glory of the LORD fills the temple.

What are we to conclude from such unusual verses? I believe that one of the reasons these verses were written was to provoke the reader into thinking in a broader manner than that which we are accustomed to. I doubt very much that many of the people of Israel would have had a working frame of reference for someone being physically lifted and moved by the Spirit, like a chess piece. I doubt that many Christians today would have such a framework, but why is this? As we have seen from Scripture, this seemed to be a regular occurrence for Ezekiel. Do we expect this sort of miraculous event? If

---

[312] Ezekiel 3:22-24
[313] Ezekiel 8:3
[314] Ezekiel 11:1-4
[315] Ezekiel 11:24-25
[316] Ezekiel 37:1-5

Ezekiel were to walk into one of our churches today, how would he be greeted? I suspect he would be looked at suspiciously, and perhaps even asked to leave. Sometimes our own piety can get in the way of what God is wanting to do in our midst.

Apart from the passages we have already looked at, there are three further references to the Spirit leading, instructing and compelling people in the in the Old Testament. Looking again at Ezekiel, we read this remarkable promise;

> "Therefore thus says the Lord GOD: Now I will restore the fortunes of Jacob and have mercy on the whole house of Israel, and I will be jealous for my holy name. They shall forget their shame and all the treachery they have practiced against me, when they dwell securely in their land with none to make them afraid, when I have brought them back from the peoples and gathered them from their enemies' lands, and through them have vindicated my holiness in the sight of many nations. Then they shall know that I am the LORD their God, because I sent them into exile among the nations and then assembled them into their own land. I will leave none of them remaining among the nations anymore. And I will not hide my face anymore from them, when I pour out my Spirit upon the house of Israel, declares the Lord GOD"[317].

Notice the intention of the LORD in this promise; He will restore their fortunes, make them forget their shame, give them security and they will know that He is God. The conduit for this happening will be when He pours out His Spirit on his people; this action of the Spirit being poured out will usher the people into all that God has in store for them. We will consider the Spirit filling and dwelling in people in the next chapter, but here we see God pouring out His Spirit to lead His people in the way they should go.

---

[317] Ezekiel 39:25-29

In the book of Isaiah, again in the context of God's people returning to their divinely appointed land, we read by what authority Isaiah is speaking these words; "For the mouth of the LORD has commanded, and His Spirit has gathered them"[318]. This is a couplet, two statements expressing one idea, which sheds some light on the link between God's commanding voice and Him sending His Spirit. This has some parallels to the work of the Trinity in the sending of Jesus; The Father sends, the Son accomplishes, the Spirit applies Jesus' victory to our lives. In Isaiah we read of the LORD commanding, and the Spirit gathering, that is, seeing that it happens. Later in Isaiah's book, we read of Isaiah proclaiming the LORD's call to Israel, with Isaiah saying that "the LORD has sent me, and His Spirit"[319]. From the context of the proceeding verses we know that the reason for the Spirit, and the prophet, being sent is to assemble the people and draw them near to God[320]. However, Isaiah is not afraid of rebuking the people of God for failing to follow the Spirit's leading and for instead making an alliance with Egypt that was "not of [Gods] Spirit."[321] The Spirit is sent to lead God's people to Himself.

**The New Testament**

Matthew, Mark and Luke all describe in the earlier chapters of their respective gospels how, after Jesus was baptized, He was led (or driven) into the wilderness by the Spirit[322], where He was tempted by the devil. Matthew specifically makes the point that His being tempted was the purpose of Jesus going into the wilderness. This makes us ask at least two questions. Firstly, why did the Spirit led Jesus into the wilderness, and secondly, why did the Spirit want Jesus to be tempted by the devil? Surely, we are to avoid confrontation with the devil at all costs[323], not actively seek it out? It

---

[318] Isaiah 34:16
[319] Isaiah 48:16
[320] Isaiah 48:14-16
[321] Isaiah 20:14
[322] Matthew 4:1, Mark 1:12, Luke 4:1
[323] James 4:7, 1 Peter 5:8-9, Ephesians 4:27, Ephesians 6:11

would be tempting to make a special case for Jesus in this regard, as we know from the vantage point of history that he lived a sinless life,[324] but this would be to ignore the fullness of Jesus' humanity. If Jesus could just 'appeal to his divinity' in a tough situation, as marvellous as that would be, He would not and could never be our fore-runner or example. No, rather we must read Jesus' life in the context of being filled with the Holy Spirit, which is how Luke describes Him[325], because this is what He passed onto His church.

One way of understanding Jesus being driven into the wilderness by the Spirit is to think of this time as a sort of 'spiritual training ground'. We could read these verses as the Spirit leading Jesus here because spending 40 days without food while being tempted would strengthen Jesus' faith for the mission which lay ahead. I love Luke's comment on this time; "...He ate nothing during those days. And when they were ended, He was hungry"[326]. Luke was never one to shy away from stating the obvious!

Notice in these passages that it is Jesus' identity that is being attacked by the devil, who tempts Jesus with phrases like; "If you are the Son of God..."[327] Jesus overcomes these challenges, interestingly enough by quoting Deuteronomy back at the devil, who subsequently leaves Him to be ministered to by angels[328]. But what of the Spirit's role in all this? The Spirit, it seems, will sometimes lead us into situations which are not comfortable, and may even be dangerous, but in these times He is always with us, has filled us and is seeking to grow us. Remember that before David fought Goliath he dealt with a lion and a bear; every battle is a training ground for future challenges and victories. Furthermore, in times of temptation, God has promised to provide a way to escape or endure temptation,[329]

---

[324] Hebrews 4:15
[325] Luke 4:1
[326] Luke 4:2
[327] Matthew 4:3, 5
[328] Matthew 4:11
[329] 1 Corinthians 10:13

which, as Jesus shows us in these wilderness passages, is to recall and claim God's truth, promises and love in the situation. Finally, Luke tells us that when Jesus returns to Galilee, He does so "in the power of the Spirit"[330]. The Spirit led Him into the wilderness, and the Spirit led Him out again.

The earlier chapters of Acts are full of references to the Holy Spirit, as we have seen in previous chapters, but surprisingly it is not until chapter eight that we see the Spirit compel someone to do something. As it happens, that person was the apostle Philip. What is interesting about the book known as 'The Acts of the Apostles', is that it actually has very little to do with the Apostles. Several of them aren't mentioned, and the majority of the second half exclusively describes Paul's ministry to the gentiles. Perhaps a more appropriate name for this Biblical book would be 'The Acts of the Holy Spirit', as this is a theme pretty much throughout.

In chapter eight, we read of the Spirit telling Philip to go and speak to the Ethiopian eunuch[331], which he does, and by explaining a passage from Isaiah, Philip leads the eunuch to faith. Immediately after Philip had baptized the man, "the Spirit of the Lord carried Philip away, and the eunuch saw him no more"[332]. Here we see a New Testament occurrence of what happened to Ezekiel; Philip was taken away by the Spirit to another place. The Greek word 'harpazo', which has been translated as 'carried away', literally means to carry off by force, or else to snatch away. It is the same word used of the birds which eat up the seed that falls on the path in Jesus' explanation of the parable of the sower[333], and Paul uses this word to describe being 'caught up' into the third heaven[334]. There is an abruptness about this word, which does not naturally lend itself to an interpretation of Philip simply walking along his way.

---

[330] Luke 4:14
[331] Acts 8:29
[332] Acts 8:39
[333] Matthew 13:19
[334] 2 Corinthians 12:2, 4

Chinese Christian Brother Yun recalls a similar occurrence in his book 'The Heavenly Man'. He describes how he was once running home from visiting another village some 6 kilometres away and, without feeling or noticing anything changing, found himself entering his home village within moments. He believes that he experienced something like what Philip did in Acts 8[335].

In Revelation, the apostle John uses a similar phrase on two occasions, where he describes himself as being "carried away in the Spirit" to a wilderness[336] and to a great high mountain[337]. The word used is 'apophero', which only occurs a few times, and essentially means 'to carry off' or 'to bring away'. The connotation of this word is very similar to 'harpazo' in the physical moving of the person in question from one place to another. From these New Testament verses, as well as from the experiences of Ezekiel, we have a Biblical basis for the Spirit physically moving someone from one place to another, which falls quite outside of what many of us would expect to be possible.

The apostle Peter uses similar language to describe his experience of God showing him that through the death and resurrection of Christ, the distinctions between clean and unclean had been removed. When he is relaying the vision he has in Acts 10 to the Jerusalem church, he describes that immediately after the vision has happened, some men sent from Cornelius in Caesarea arrived at his door[338]. Peter tells the story like this; "The Spirit told me to go with them, making no distinction"[339]. Here we see a direct prompting of the Spirit for Peter to forsake his former prejudices and to accompany these strangers to their gentile master to share the Gospel with them. It seems reasonable to assume that the vision was perfectly

---

[335] Brother Yun and P. Hattaway, 'The Heavenly Man', Oxford: Monarch Books, 2009, pp38-39
[336] Revelation 17:3
[337] Revelation 21:10
[338] Acts 10:17-23, Acts 11:11
[339] Acts 11:12

timed by God to shake Peter up enough to follow the Spirit and not his racist heritage.

A favourite verse of mine is Acts 13:1, which describes the church in Antioch as having both prophets and teachers. The next verse tells us that while this mighty church was fasting and worshipping, the Holy Spirit told them to set apart Barnabus and Saul for a specific work to which they had been called[340]. The church's response was to fast and pray about this, but ultimately to release them to do this work. This is a wonderful picture of faithfulness on the part of the Antioch church, to send two of their five named leaders off on an unknown quest, but they did so in obedience to the Holy Spirit's call.[341] Three chapters later, in the run up to when Paul and Timothy receive a vision of the Macedonian man, they venture through the regions of Phrygia and Galatia in modern Turkey, because they had been "forbidden by the Holy Spirit to speak the word in Asia"[342]. The next verse tells us that they also attempted to go to Bithynia, but "the Spirit of Jesus did not allow them".

What is not clear from the text is why or how the Spirit prevents Paul and Timothy from going to Asia or Bithynia. It would seem that the Spirit, being fully God, was here somehow restraining Paul and Timothy from visiting these regions. Perhaps He arranged for some off-putting circumstance to arise which would have hindered their travel. However, given what Paul was willing to endure for the Gospel[343], it's hard to imagine what these circumstances might be. Alternatively, perhaps the Spirit was so impressing on their hearts that they were not to go to these places that they couldn't help but obey. However, we must also see the providence of God in this situation. The rest of the book of Acts could have looked very different had Paul and Timothy been allowed to visit Asia and Bithynia; perhaps the purpose of sending these men down another

---

[340] Acts 13:2
[341] Acts 13:4
[342] Acts 16:6
[343] 2 Corinthians 11:24-28

path was for Paul to ultimately end up in Rome, so as to spread the Gospel as far and wide as the Roman empire stretched.

In Acts 19 we find Paul 'resolving in the Spirit' to go to Jerusalem via Macedonia and Achaia, which serves as a healthy example of how a Christian should make a decision[344]. We are not told exactly what he did to 'resolve in the Spirit', but he was clearly not making his travel or missional arrangements exclusively out of his own intellect. Perhaps he had learned from what happened in Acts 13 that if the Spirit doesn't want something to happen then it simply wouldn't happen. Maybe Paul had realised something in his spirit that if he is to be truly Christ-like, he must include the Holy Spirit in all his doings. So, rather than just deciding to do something and hoping the Spirit would accompany him and bless his actions, in Acts 19 he includes the Spirit in his decision making; having communion with the living God by His Spirit who dwells within.

Later in Acts, when Paul is addressing the leaders of the Ephesian church, he explains that he is about to head to Jerusalem, not knowing what will await him there. He says that he goes "constrained by the Spirit"[345], as it is translated in the ESV. The KJV renders this as 'I go bound in the Spirit', while the NIV says, 'And now, compelled by the Spirit, I am going to Jerusalem'. I am not sure that the ESV's phrasing of 'constrained by the Spirit' is the best translation here, as 'constrain' has connotations of preventing someone from doing something, which is exactly the opposite of what Paul is saying. However, the Greek word in question is *'deo'*, which is used 44 times in the New Testament, and is always translated as being bound or tied, either literally ('I was bound in chains') or metaphorically ('I am bound to my wife'). In this case, the choice of the word *'deo'* seems to be conveying more than many of our translations would want to allow. I believe the best translation is the KJV's 'I go bound in the Spirit', as this is equally faithful to the

---

[344] Acts 19:21
[345] Acts 20:22

connotation of the original Greek word, but also makes sense in light of Paul's description of what lies ahead for him.

He goes on to say, in the very next verse, that the Spirit has testified to him that nothing but hardships await him in every city[346]. These aren't the most comforting words the Spirit has ever imparted, but they seem to have been liberating for Paul, because he goes on to explain that he no longer counts his life as worth anything if forfeiting it means he can finish his ministry[347]. Paul was so committed to his ministry that he didn't care what faced him. He felt so strongly that he describes it as being 'bound by the Spirit', as though with physical ropes; such is the strength of the conviction that this is what he must do and that he will not be alone in it.

Curiously, in the very next chapter Paul has left Ephesus and has arrived at Tyre on his way to Jerusalem. In Tyre, Paul and his companions stay with some members of the church there, and they begin to tell Paul 'through the Spirit' not to go to Jerusalem[348]. This raises a question; if Paul was so sure that the Spirit was telling him to go to Jerusalem when he was in Ephesus, why were the disciples at Tyre telling him "through the Spirit" not to go? Had either Paul or the Tyre disciples misheard or misunderstood the Spirit? Did the Spirit change His mind between Paul leaving Ephesus and arriving at Tyre? Or was He wrong on one of these occasions?

If any of these possibilities are true, this would punch some sizable holes in evangelical theology. However, I believe we can reconcile these two apparently contradictory statements, both of which claim to be 'by the Spirit'. If we look slightly further ahead of the passage about Tyre, we find Paul coming to Caesarea and staying with Philip the evangelist[349]. While Paul was there, a prophet called Agabus came down from Judea, took Paul's belt and bound his own hands

---

[346] Acts 20:23
[347] Acts 20:24
[348] Acts 21:2-3
[349] Acts 21:8

and feet, saying that this is what awaits the owner of this belt in Jerusalem[350]. At this, those who were there, including Acts' author Luke, urged him and pleaded with him not to go to Jerusalem. Paul would not be persuaded, and he ultimately does go to Jerusalem.

This incident in Philip's house with Agabus the prophet, and the reaction of those who heard the prophesy, throws some light on how to understand the apparent inconsistencies we mentioned previously. Notice how both Agabus and the disciples at Tyre end up telling Paul that he should not journey to Jerusalem. I believe that the Spirit had revealed to the Tyre disciples, to Agabus and to Paul what would happen in Jerusalem[351], but that Paul had the superior revelation because he, in essence, saw past the hardships to the fruit that would come of it. I would suggest that the Spirit revealed different amount of information about the future to different people. The Tyre disciples and Agabus received accurate information; they just didn't receive all of the available information. Remember, Paul has "resolved in the Spirit"[352] to go to Jerusalem, regardless of the cost, for the glory of proclaiming the gospel was a greater prize than even saving his own life. This could serve as a lesson to contemporary churches; when seeking the Spirit for direction on something, we should keep on seeking even after an answer becomes apparent, as there may be more.

There is an imperative that Paul is modelling here; he writes to the Roman church that those who are led by the Spirit of God are sons of God. This means that those who are Christians are led by the Spirit, and, as we established in chapter 7, being a son of God isn't only for certain types of Christians, it is a right given to all who call on His name[353]. The Spirit leads us into worship, to glory in the victory of Christ and to put no confidence in the flesh. This means

---

350 Acts 21:11
351 Acts 20:23, 21:4, 21:11
352 Acts 19:21
353 John 1:12

that the Spirit leads us to lift our eyes to focus on the things of heaven, as opposed to the things of earth[354].

## Conclusions

Having looked at what the Bible has to say about this subject, what difference can we see this making to our lives? If we read the Bible to simply get information, we miss the point entirely. Rather, we must allow the Bible to bring about transformation in our lives by letting it influence our faith and practice. Firstly, as we've learned from Ezekiel, something being unusual from our perspective does not make it wrong. Ezekiel was a man very much in tune with the Spirit of God, and God required such strange things of him, as well as showing him the weird wonders of heaven. We should not be afraid of people or events which we find unusual, as they may well be a glimpse of something of heaven which we could only dream of.

Secondly, as we have seen in the life of Isaiah and from our understanding of the Trinity, when the Spirit leads you in a direction or into a situation, the ultimate destination of the journey He leads you on is to God himself. The Spirit is sent to us to make us feel and believe like we are sons of God; sons who are drawn to their loving Father. The Spirit leads God's people to Himself, and indeed He also leads people who don't yet know God as 'Father' to Himself, as we will see in chapter 10.

Thirdly, from Jesus' time in the wilderness we see that when the Spirit leads people into times of difficulty, He also leads them out again in power. I don't imagine for a minute that Jesus' divinity meant that His time in the wilderness was any less difficult than a 'wilderness' situation we might face. Rather, as Luke describes, Jesus was "full of the Spirit"[355] when He went into the wilderness, and returned from the wilderness "in the power of the Spirit"[356]. Because

---

[354] Philippians 3:3
[355] Luke 4:1
[356] Luke 4:14

we now have the Spirit living in us, we can be assured that if the Spirit leads us into a 'wilderness' situation, He will just as surely lead us out of it again.

Finally, the missionary journeys of Paul beg us to question whether we include the Holy Spirit in our decision making. There are, it seems, ways to make decisions which may appear wise in the eyes of men, but do not have divine backing. On the other hand, there are ways of making decisions by waiting on, listening to and trusting in the Holy Spirit. This is the way Paul made decisions, by 'resolving' in the Spirit, which isn't necessarily a speedy process. Furthermore, this way of decision making may look like foolishness to onlookers, as going to Jerusalem was for Paul. However, resolving in the Spirit to do something looks past the circumstances to what God is doing in the situation. This should extend to all aspects of a believer's life; when an important decision is to be made, we should appeal to the Spirit of wisdom and of revelation[357] to lead us in our decision making.

---

[357] Ephesians 1:17

# Eight

# The Spirit Fills and Indwells

## ✳✳✳

Thus far in this book, we've made many references to the Spirit living in the believer, but without really exploring what this means, what it looks like and what the Biblical basis for it is. The idea of the Spirit living in the believer will be quite familiar to many Christians, while others won't have given it much thought. Does the Spirit of the living God really live *in* me? How can that be? As with everything in the Christian life, we must base our faith and practise on what Scripture says, to which we now turn.

### The Old Testament

The idea of the Spirit living in the believer is a very New Testament concept. Because of this, the Old Testament has little to say about this idea, because until the ministry of Jesus, the Spirit resided in the Holy of Holies in the temple in Jerusalem, or before that in the tabernacle[358]. However, there are some Old Testament passages which speak about the Spirit living inside people. In Genesis 6, before the narrative about Noah and the flood, we find a curious passage about the Nephilim. 'Nephilim' is a transliteration of the Hebrew word for 'giant', and appears only here and in Numbers 13, where Israelite spies were sent to the land of Canaan to spy out the

---

[358] It should be noted that I am referring to the specific and manifest presence of God, as opposed to the general presence of God. Old Testament worshippers would be required to go to a particular geographical place in order to meet with God in a personal way. In a more general sense, God is the Lord of all the earth, and as such He is present in the whole universe (Psalm 97:5, Joshua 3:11, Micah 4:13, Zechariah 4:15, etc.)

land. They report back to Moses and Caleb that "And there we saw the Nephilim (the sons of Anak, who come from the Nephilim), and we seemed to ourselves like grasshoppers, and so we seemed to them"[359].

Understanding what or who the Nephilim were is not an easy task, and is certainly outside the scope of this book, but the verse in this passage that refers to the Spirit records God saying that His Spirit shall not abide in man forever, for he is flesh, and limiting his days to 120 years[360]. The Hebrew word for 'abide' here is *'diyn'*, but translating this word has been problematic, because at least 14 English translations, including the New International Version and the King James Version, translate this as 'strive with' instead of 'abide in'. Conversely, some 23 English translations render this word as 'dwell in' or something similar. The issue is further confounded by the etymology (origin and use) of the word *'diyn'*, which seems to be exclusively concerned with judging, pleading or governing. Why, then, does the ESV, along with at least 22 other English translations render this word as 'abide'? It could be because of the connotation of 'governing', that being, God's Spirit will not govern man forever, because he is mortal.

It remains a mystery, and many greater Bible scholars than I have been found wanting for a satisfactory understanding[361]. However these verses are to be read, for our purposes we can say that the Spirit will not strive or abide in man forever. This passage is the preface to the mighty flood sent to rid the land of moral abominations, and so we can conclude that God's Spirit was withdrawn from dwelling in 'all men' for eternity, presumably as a result of Adam's original sin and of this moral decadence. This may be a commentary about the 'fallout' from Adam's original sin, so that the LORD was not so much removing His Spirit from man at this

---

[359] Numbers 13:33
[360] Genesis 6:3
[361] See F.F. Bruce (ed), *'New International Bible Commentary'*, Michigan: Zondervan, 1979, p120

moment, but rather commenting that the Spirit had already been removed, as a prelude to the flood. It would make sense for the author to emphasise that the blessings of eternal life were not present in the people who were involved in extreme examples of sinful behaviour, or else the flood would have been a blessing, sweeping countless people into heaven rather than imposing judgement on their sin. As Proverbs says, "The wicked is overthrown through his evildoing, but the righteous finds refuge in his death"[362]. The Spirit of the LORD dwells with the righteous, and so we can view this verse as making a clear distinction between the unrighteous person and the righteous person, which we see in Noah.

When the ark is seen as a 'type of Christ'[363], that is, an Old Testament precursor to what Christ would achieve on the cross, this makes even more sense; if salvation comes from Christ only, to offer salvation apart from faith in Christ (or the ark, in the Genesis parallel) would be contrary to the message of the Gospel. The Gospel tells us that apart from Christ a person is in dire need; the ark is a picture of this, so for God's Spirit to dwell in 'men' forever, meaning 'humanity', irrespective of their relationship to Him and His standards, would be unacceptable.

The remainder of the Old Testament references to the Spirit filling or dwelling within someone are from Ezekiel. As we saw extensively in the last chapter, Ezekiel had many wonderful encounters with God which may seem bizarre from an earthly perspective. Two of these instances use the phrase 'the Spirit entered into me and set me on my feet'[364], showing us that when the Spirit compels Ezekiel to do something, He does so by 'entering into him'. Similarly, later on in this book, we read of God telling Israel that He will put His Spirit in them so that they will be able to follow His statutes and rules[365]. This was one of the aims of Pentecost; God dwelling inside people

---

[362] Proverbs 14:32
[363] See Hebrews 11:7, Luke 17:26 and 1 Peter 3:20
[364] Ezekiel 2:2, 3:24
[365] Ezekiel 36:27

enables them to live out a godly life. Ezekiel's vision of the valley of dry bones is equally telling of God's intentions for his people;

> "I will put my Spirit within you, and you shall live, and I will place you in your own land. Then you shall know that I am the LORD"[366].

Here we see God promising His people that His Spirit will live within them, another precursor to Pentecost. But more than just being a messianic promise, this has life-giving implications; "...you shall live and I will place you in your own land." These words show us that the Spirit filling someone and living in someone has implications for the desires of that person's heart. In this case it was the desire to live, and to do so in their own land, but the ultimate goal of having the Spirit living inside of you is the final part of this verse; "Then you shall know that I am the LORD". The Spirit living in us shows us more of God.

## The Gospels

In the opening chapter of Matthew's gospel, he describes how the birth of Jesus came about. Matthew describes twice in the same sentence how Jesus was conceived. He affirms that Mary was found to be 'with child' before she and Joseph slept together[367], but also that this child was 'from the Holy Spirit'. This clarifies a misconception that some people believe about Mary; she was not simply unfaithful to Joseph. This was certainly how Joseph interpreted the situation, but an angel makes it plain to Joseph that he has wrongly construed what has happened[368]. By having two explanations in the same verse, Matthew is eliminating all possible doubt about whether Jesus was conceived 'from the Holy Spirit'. There is a definite element of a creative miracle here, which we will discuss in the next chapter, but Matthew is clear that what was

---

[366] Ezekiel 37:14
[367] Matthew 1:18
[368] Matthew 1:20

happening in Mary's womb was of the Holy Spirit. When Gabriel appears to Mary to explain what is going to happen, he tells her that;

> "The Holy Spirit will come upon you, and the power of the Most High will overshadow you; therefore the child to be born will be called holy—the Son of God"[369].

We discussed in the previous chapter how Jesus was 'full of the Holy Spirit' as he entered and exited the wilderness after his baptism[370]; it seems that even Jesus' conception was blessed by the Spirit. The Eastern Orthodox and Roman Catholic 'hail Mary' phrase reads "Blessed art thou amongst women and blessed is the fruit of thy womb". While I don't believe that Mary is worthy of worship in the same manner that Jesus is, she is certainly to be honoured and seen as a wonderful example of faithfulness to God amidst difficult circumstances. The 'hail Mary' phrase is taken from Luke 1:42, and, for all intents and purposes, seems to be entirely accurate; no other woman has carried the Son of God in her womb, and the fruit of her womb is certainly blessed. Notice that in the previous verse, when the pregnant Mary greets the pregnant Elizabeth, the embryonic John the Baptist leaps in her womb, and Elizabeth is filled with the Spirit. The advent of John and Jesus heralds a new phase of people of all walks of life being filled with the Spirit.

The birth narratives of John the Baptist also show us the Spirit filling someone, even from his mother's womb. This is important, as while John the Baptist was certainly an important figure in bridging the old and new covenants, he was not fully divine like Jesus was. If we make separate categories for everyone who has a meaningful role in Scripture, including Jesus, we essentially exclude ourselves from doing or experiencing anything Scripture says. This would be saying something like; 'That experience was all well and good for Paul, but he was a mighty apostle and I'm not. I couldn't possible expect to

---

369 Luke 1:35
370 Mark 1:10

have such an experience.' This effectively means that whatever Scripture says about salvation, gifts or an experiential God is rendered null and void as far as the contemporary church is concerned, as salvation, gifts and experiences are all contained within the Bible. Rather, we should view ourselves as being in the same category as everyone in the Bible except Jesus, because He is sinless man and fully God while we are not. Having said that, because the Christian is 'in Christ' and can be filled with the Spirit in the same way that Christ was, how Jesus walked by the Spirit is how He has enabled us to walk by the Spirit.

Fortunately, Scripture makes no such distinctions, as we can see in the life of John the Baptist. We read in Luke 1 that an angel accosted Zechariah while he was in the temple and explains that the forerunner to the messiah would be Zechariah's son and would;

> "...be great before the Lord. And he must not drink wine or strong drink, and he will be filled with the Holy Spirit, even from his mother's womb"[371].

The angel makes several characteristics very clear about John the Baptist. Firstly, he should not drink alcohol, presumably to be without blame before the religious institutions of the day; John's ministry was unconventional, and perhaps abstaining from alcohol was a way of avoiding unjust criticism. Also, Jesus mentions John's abstinence from alcohol in comparison to His own liberty regarding it. Jesus recalls how the crowds complained about John not drinking alcohol, calling him demon possessed, but then the same people call Jesus a glutton and a drunkard for eating and drinking, but ultimately the wisest course is revealed through one's deeds[372].

The second characteristic concerning John was that many will rejoice at his birth because he would herald the day of the LORD. Thirdly, he would be filled with the Spirit, even from his mother's womb. This

---

[371] Luke 1:15
[372] Matthew 11:18-19

is important and somewhat unprecedented. While, as we have seen earlier in this chapter, there had been people who had been filled with the Spirit, and of course after Pentecost many thousands were filled with the Spirit, for someone to be filled with the Spirit *from their mother's womb* had never been seen before.

We must ask ourselves whether we believe that John the Baptist was filled with the Spirit in Elizabeth's womb, but then after he was born ceased to be filled with the Spirit. This seems unlikely, given the ministry he had, and as such it would seem appropriate to say that he was full of the Holy Spirit throughout his life. Perhaps this is the reason that Jesus described him as being the greatest who has been born of women, and that even the least in the kingdom of heaven is greater than he[373]: John was a prototype, the first to be filled with the Spirit for his whole life. The question of whether a child born to Christian parents is automatically 'saved' is on-going, and while I tend to lean towards believing that such children are, as it were, 'safe in their parents faith', this is based mainly on my belief in God's justice and mercy, as opposed to any concrete Biblical evidence. That being said, I do believe that anyone can experience the Spirit from a very young age, and as we have seen in the example of John the Baptist, I also believe that someone can be *filled with* the Spirit from being very young, even if they are unsure what this means.

**Three Churches**

While there are hints at what being filled with the Spirit means in the Old Testament and the Gospels, it is in Acts and in the Epistles that we find the most information about this topic. On the day of Pentecost, the disciples were all together in the same place when the Holy Spirit came like the sound of wind from Heaven, with tongues of fire resting on the disciples and each one being filled with the Holy Spirit[374]. Notice in this passage that this experience wasn't limited simply to the twelve, but rather it was the entire church that

---

[373] Matthew 11:11
[374] Acts 2:1-4

experienced it. This was about 120 people[375], and Luke makes it clear that tongues of fire rested on 'each one' of them, and that 'they were all' filled with the Holy Spirit. This was not an exclusive event, actually quite the opposite. On the day of Pentecost every single Christian was filled with the Holy Spirit. The result of this was that they began to speak in tongues, Peter preached powerfully and three thousand people were added to their number. Also, because of the fact that Jerusalem was home to people from a multitude of different nations, the people who were added to the church made the church international. To put this another way, the combination of being filled with the Spirit, the outpouring of spiritual gifts and Spirit-empowered preaching caused the first church to increase 25-fold and become multi-national in one day. Can the modern church afford to ignore this implication?

While some may contend that this was a one-time event, this is just not the case. When Peter is in the house of Cornelius in Acts 10, even before he has finished preaching to them, the Holy Spirit falls on those gathered and they begin 'speaking in tongues and extolling God'[376]. For Peter, this was revolutionary, as the people he was speaking to were gentiles, and yet they had received the Spirit in an identical way to the original Jewish believers. He cannot help but be convinced that gentiles are just as equally admissible into God's kingdom as Jews are. When explaining this to the Jerusalem church, he describes this by saying that, "as [he] began to speak, the Holy Spirit fell on [the gentiles] just as on us at the beginning.[377]" He was taken aback by the similarity this event had with Pentecost, and concluded that the gospel was available to anyone, regardless of their race.

I once heard a recording of Tim Keller preaching a very good sermon on this passage; however his perspective was that the Spirit filling

---

[375] Acts 1:15
[376] Acts 10:44 - 46
[377] Acts 11:15

the gentiles on this occasion was a sign for Peter about there now being no distinction between Jew and Gentile in Christ. Keller reads this passage as a manual for Christians to not distinguish along racial lines. While this is certainly one application we can draw from these verses, to see the filling by the Holy Spirit as incidental is to ignore what actually transpired. We can forget that what we read of in Scripture are actual events which really occurred to real people: they are not just helpful illustrations with which to punctuate our ethical frameworks. These gentiles were real people who experienced the Holy Spirit filling them in a real way.

As if this wasn't sufficient evidence to bolster the case for the necessity of being filled with the Holy Spirit today, we read in Acts 19 of when Paul found himself in Ephesus. When he came across some disciples, he immediately asked them if they received the Spirit when they believed. Whether or not this was the first thing he said to them, or just that this is the most important detail that Luke thought to record is not the point; Paul made it an issue of importance to enquire into their experience of the Holy Spirit[378]. Note here that these people were believers; Luke describes them as 'disciples' and they confess that they have been baptised, albeit into John's baptism of repentance. The specific reference to these people as 'believers' tells us that being 'baptised' with the Spirit is not an automatic happening when someone believes in Jesus. Rather, these are two different phenomena. These people in Ephesus believed in Jesus and had been baptized in water, but upon their own admission had not even heard that the Holy Spirit existed. This shows us that someone can be a Christian but not be filled with the Holy Spirit.

The response Paul gives to this situation is equally telling. He is anything but apathetic about this, and proceeds to point out their theological oversight, before baptising them in the name of Jesus and laying hands on them. As he was doing this, the Holy Spirit comes upon them and they began speaking in tongues and

---

[378] Acts 19:1-2

prophesying. Paul does not say that this is an area for discussion, to be debated about or that each church has its different way of doing things. This was an imperative for him, something that he did not want to see this church do without. Here we can see a similar pattern again to that of Pentecost; theological exposition, being filled with the Holy Spirit and the outpouring of spiritual gifts. There is a strong case here, drawn from the three events of Pentecost, the house of Cornelius and here in Ephesus for this to be the normal experience of churches.

## Paul's Story

Perhaps one of the reasons Paul was so fervently in favour of churches being filled with the Spirit was because this phenomenon was so instrumental in his life. While he was still known as Saul, he was on his way to Damascus with the sole purpose of arresting and transporting Christians to trials in Jerusalem, when the risen Christ appears to him and knocks him to the ground, blinding him in the process[379]. He needed to be led by the hand and refused food and water for several days, until a disciple named Ananias bravely went to pray for him to receive his sight and to have him filled with the Holy Spirit. As soon as this happens, Saul regains his sight and is baptised[380]. It is a great comfort to realise that it is not only Jesus who appears to Saul on the road, but it is also Jesus who commissions Ananias to go and pray for Saul's sight to be restored and for him to be filled with the Holy Spirit[381]. Being filled with the Spirit is Jesus' idea.

We read a curiously similar account of Paul being filled with the Spirit in Acts 13, where he harshly rebukes a magician called Elymas for "making crooked the straight paths of the Lord"[382]. After this, Paul pronounces that Elymas will be blind and unable to see the sun for a

---

[379] Acts 9:1-8
[380] Acts 9:10-18
[381] Acts 9:10
[382] Acts 13:8-10

while, which happens, and he goes about seeking someone to lead him by the hand[383]. There are several points of similarity between this and what happened to Paul on the way to Damascus; being filled with the Spirit is mentioned, albeit with different outcomes, both are struck blind and both need to be led around by the hand. Also, it would seem that both of these are struck down blind as punishment for a great crime against the faith; Paul for arresting and murdering Christians and Elymas for seeking to turn the Proconsul away from the faith[384]. The difference is that we don't know what happened to Elymas, while we do know what happened to Paul. Given the similarities between them, we could suppose that the same redemption that was offered to Paul was also offered to Elyman, and could hope that Elymas also found someone to lead him by the hand, lead him to Christ and ensure that he was filled with the Holy Spirit.

**Godly lives**

At several points throughout Acts there are instances where certain people are described in very positive tones, an example of this being when the disciples are choosing deacons in Acts 6. The twelve gather all the disciples and instruct them that there needs to be a provision made to meet the material needs of their widows, but that they shouldn't neglect the preaching of the word to do so. So, they tell the church to pick from themselves seven men who are well thought of, and who are full of wisdom and full of the Spirit[385]. Interestingly, the seven who are chosen were not chosen by the twelve, but rather, as verse 3 says, they were to 'pick out from among [them]' those who were to serve, who would be in turn 'set before the apostles' to be prayed for[386]. There is an autonomy given to the church by their leaders to choose who would serve them. We could learn from this; not all decisions need to come from church

---

[383] Acts 13:11
[384] Acts 13:8
[385] Acts 6:1-4
[386] Acts 6:6

leadership. Those in a church should all responsible for the decisions made.

The criteria used to choose the deacons were that they were full of wisdom, full of the Spirit and of good repute. The deacon who is most noted in Acts is Steven, who is specifically mentioned as being a man "full of faith and of the Holy Spirit"[387], but who meets a martyr's death. This is a particularly flattering description, and certainly one that could be aspired to. Stephen is picked, and named, first among the deacons with specific reference to his faith and him being Spirit-filled. In the next two verses, Luke records that the church continued to increase in number[388], and also that Stephen was doing great signs and wonders among the people, being full of grace and power[389]. Even as he faced his death, Stephen is described as being full of the Holy Spirit, and praying for those who were about to kill him[390], clearly imitating Christ's example. Stephen's testimony shows us that being filled with the Spirit isn't just something that is necessary for the leaders of a church or those who are preaching; rather anyone who is serving needs God's power to do so, something confirmed by the Jerusalem church's assessment of Barnabas when sending him to Antioch[391]. The practical work done by the deacons and other non-elders was empowered by the Spirit dwelling within, even up until the point of death.

**The Temple of God**

All this is especially necessary for today's church, whose ministries have never been needed more. However, we still are left with one very pressing question; what does it *mean* to be filled with the Spirit and to have the Spirit dwelling inside us? What does that look like?

---

[387] Acts 6:5
[388] Acts 6:7
[389] Acts 6:8
[390] Acts 7:55, 60
[391] Acts 11:24

Several of the New Testament epistles describe, using the imagery of a temple, what this means for believers.

While there are several metaphors in the Bible for what the church is and should look like, the idea of the temple of God takes precedent. Paul's legendary eighth chapter of Romans tells us that those who are of the flesh cannot please God[392]. This might be troubling to read, as my body is made of flesh, but this isn't what Paul is saying. He is talking about those who *live* according to the flesh, that is, those who are not in Christ. He goes on to say that Christians are not in the flesh, but are in the Spirit, "if in fact the Spirit of God lives in you"[393]. He continues by saying that, in light of the fact that we have the Spirit of Him who raised Christ from the dead living in us, we can be assured that Christ will bring life to our mortal bodies by the Spirit living in us[394]. While Paul doesn't use the word 'temple' in these verses, the idea of the Spirit living in us is certainly floated as a truth to be embraced and that through this we can live in a manner which is beyond 'living by the flesh'.

The first occurrence of the phrase 'the temple of the Holy Spirit' is found in 1 Corinthians 3, where Paul reassures the Corinthian church by saying;

> "Do you not know that you are God's temple and that God's Spirit dwells in you? If anyone destroys God's temple, God will destroy him. For God's temple is holy, and you are that temple"[395].

These are words of comfort, essentially saying that because we are God's temple, we can rely on God to look after us and look out for us. This does not mean that we are prevented from harm, because Jesus says that a servant is not greater than his master, and that His

---

[392] Romans 8:8
[393] Romans 8:9
[394] Romans 8:11
[395] 1 Corinthians 3:16-17

followers will be persecuted as He was persecuted[396]. So what is Paul meaning here? My grandfather was conscripted into service in the Second World War and although I never met him, my dad has told me that he would hold onto what is written in Psalm 91, which includes lines like;

> "He who dwells in the shelter of the Most High will abide in the shadow of the Almighty. I will say to the LORD, "My refuge and my fortress, my God, in whom I trust." ... A thousand may fall at your side, ten thousand at your right hand, but it will not come near you"[397].

My grandfather later spent several years in a prisoner of war camp, and although he survived the war he was a different man when he returned home, like millions of others. As it turned out, my grandfather lived through the war, but there were occasions where he was literally moments from death. If he had indeed died, what would his family have made of his beloved Psalm 91? Can this psalm, or the passage in 1 Corinthians 3, be used as a promise from God to never let anything happen to the person who believes it? I suspect it really depends on what we mean by 'let anything happen'. 1 Corinthians 3 tells us that 'if anyone destroys God's temple, God will destroy them'. This is not a guarantee of physical safety, although there is an assurance of eternal safety. Rather, this is expressing how God feels about His temple, His people. Also, we should remember that this was not given as a warning to those who would seek to harm the temple, but rather was given as a promise to those who belong to God; we are God's temple because God the Spirit dwells within us.

Later in the same letter, Paul uses the temple analogy when discussing sexual immorality. He instructs the church to flee 'sexual immorality'[398], which is probably a poor translation as it doesn't

---

[396] John 15:20
[397] Psalm 91:1-2, 7
[398] 1 Corinthians 6:18

factor in the gravity and scope of the sin involved. The word from which this is translated is *'porneia'*, where we get our word 'pornography' from, and is the act of having sex with someone, or something, you are not married to. The translation of this word is 'sexual immorality' in the NIV and ESV, and while this was intended to be a catch-all phrase as opposed to having a list within a sentence, it does leave unanswered the question of 'what is sexual immorality?' The original word has no ambiguity, and I believe that breaking up the flow of a sentence is a small price to pay to prevent faithful people from misconstruing God's word.

What is interesting for our purposes is that the argument Paul presented in order to convince the Corinthians not to have sex with prostitutes was that their bodies were the temple of the Holy Spirit; they were not their own, they were bought at a price, and so they were to glorify God in their bodies[399]. The living God dwelling within the believer by the Holy Spirit is a wonderful truth, which comes to us for free, but it being free does not mean it was inexpensive. Christ died a brutal death, enduring the wrath of God as well as the physical agony of crucifixion, in order to make us the temple of the Holy Spirit. If we dig slightly into the Greek for the word 'temple', we learn that this word, *'naos'*, is used of the sanctuary, which consisted of the Holy Place and the Holy of Holies, which is where the presence of God dwelt in the old covenant. God has made us to be the place where His very presence dwells; He has made us His home.

Paul uses a similar argument with regard to drunkenness in Ephesians 5, where he tells the church not to get drunk on wine, which leads to debauchery, but rather to be filled with the Spirit[400]. Debauchery is something of an archaic word, but it essentially means having lax morals and indulging in sensual vices. Paul discourages getting drunk, which leads to this immorality, but compels them to

---

[399] 1 Corinthians 6:19-20
[400] Ephesians 5:18

be filled with the Holy Spirit as an alternative. Being the temple of the Holy Spirit leads to a holy lifestyle.

The apostle John says that "whoever keeps His commandments abides in God, and God in him"[401]. Almost as if he were anticipating the question, he immediately goes on to say that we can know that God lives in us is by the Spirit, whom He has given us[402]. He says basically the same thing in the following chapter, where he implores his readers to love one another;

> "...if we love one another, God abides in us and His love is perfected in us. By this we know that we abide in Him and He in us, because He has given us of His Spirit"[403].

The Spirit testifies with us that we love one another. Love is the currency of, and key to, the kingdom of God; if we love one another God abides in us and his love is perfected in us. We know this by the Spirit, and we obey His commandments by the same Spirit and by the love of God within us. John records Jesus as saying so in his gospel[404], and here John is reminding his readers several decades later of what Jesus said. You cannot obey your way into the love of God; you must love your way into obedience. This order of doing things is contrary to human nature, but hundreds of years before either John of Jesus were born, Ezekiel prophesied that this would happen;

> "I will give you a new heart, and a new spirit I will put within you. And I will remove the heart of stone from your flesh and give you a heart of flesh. And I will put my Spirit within you, and cause you to walk in my statutes and be careful to obey my rules"[405].

---

[401] 1 John 3:24
[402] Ibid.
[403] 1 John 4:12-13
[404] John 14:15-17

It is not within the capabilities of humans, apart from the indwelling of God by His Spirit, to observe any, let alone all, of the rules. In order to live in the way God requires of His people we need His help and His nearness. The prophet Jeremiah writes similar promises about the new covenant that was to come;

> "Behold, the days are coming, declares the LORD, when I will make a new covenant with the house of Israel and the house of Judah... I will put my law within them, and I will write it on their hearts. And I will be their God, and they shall be my people"[406].

The idea that you or I or anyone can fulfil the law apart from the help of God, even if we know intellectually that we are saved by grace and we can add nothing to that, is preposterous. We need God's intervention to do so. The roots of this reality are buried deep in the Old Testament, and see their fruition through what Christ bought on the cross; God living in us by His Spirit.

Two letters by the apostle Paul contain verses which might cause us to re-assess our understanding of 'God's temple'. We read in Ephesians 2 that "...In him you also are being built together into a dwelling place for God by the Spirit"[407] and in 2 Timothy 2; "By the Holy Spirit who dwells within us..."[408]. What is interesting about these verses is that the emphasis is put on the collective nature of God's temple. Notice the language used in Ephesians 2; "you are being built together..." This points to a collaborative effort, something is happening in the midst of God's people in a way that is different from one believer alone. Paul's second letter to Timothy also makes reference to the Spirit who dwells within 'us', presumably meaning Paul and Timothy. Now of course we could read this as 'the Spirit lives in you and the Spirit also lives in me' as two separate

---

405 Ezekiel 36:26-27
406 Jeremiah 31:31, 33
407 Ephesians 2:22
408 2 Timothy 2:14

statements, but the verse from Ephesians 2 seems to undermine this thinking. Ephesians is saying that, while the Spirit individually dwells within me, I am being built together with other believers to be a dwelling place for God. This is a wonderful picture of the church; each brick is important, but the whole is greater than the sum of the parts. Or, to put it another way, we can do more together than we can apart. Peter put it like this;

> "As you come to Him, a living stone... you yourselves like living stones are being built up as a spiritual house"[409].

I believe in two equal truths about this matter; the Spirit of God dwells in me and the Spirit of God dwells in the church. I also believe that this is an on-going reality, and that as we walk through our Christian lives this will become more 'real' both personally and collectively. One of my favourite verses in the Bible is found in its very last chapter, only a few verses from the end, and shows us the goal of the Spirit living within us; "The Spirit and the bride say 'come'."[410] There is such harmony among the church, Christ's bride, that we can say 'come Lord Jesus' in the same voice as the Spirit. This is the unity between church and Spirit in the new heavens and the new earth, and is certainly something to pray towards.

## Conclusions

While we have surveyed more than fifty Scriptures, it would be untrue to say that the idea of God Himself living inside me wasn't still something of a mystery. That being said, this comes with the territory of being a Christian; we live with the mysteries of God. Isaiah tells us that God's ways and thoughts are higher and dissimilar to our own[411], which is a comfort in a way. If God were small enough for us to fully understand, He would not be big enough

---

[409] 1 Peter 2:4-5
[410] Revelation 22:17
[411] Isaiah 55:8-9

for us to fully trust[412]. However, what He has revealed through His Son, His Word and His Spirit do at least give us something to go by.

What we can say from this chapter is that being filled with the Spirit is a normal part of the Christian life. It is not something reserved for 'special Christians', as if such a ludicrous category existed, nor for the early church or even for a particular branch of the church. In Scripture we see being filled with the Spirit as a standard part of being a Christian, and as a priority of the apostles. Can we, in churches in the 21st century, make this doctrine any less of a priority than the original followers of Christ did with any kind of Biblical integrity?

Secondly, we can say that being filled with the Spirit is necessary for all Christian work, not just those in senior leadership. The examples of Steven and Barnabas in Acts show us that the priority given by the first church was to seek out people who were 'full of wisdom and the Holy Spirit' in order to undertake the ministries of the church, in this case being deacons. Serving a Spirit-filled church necessitates being a Spirit-filled servant.

Thirdly, if we were to summarise the Bible's teaching on this topic, and therefore of this chapter, in just a few words, we could say that 'being filled with the Spirit is having God living inside you, enabling you to live a holy life and to love your brother and neighbour'. That is the point and purpose of the doctrine; anything else which results from being filled with the Spirit is a bonus. The fruit of the Spirit[413] is the result of being filled with the Spirit.

Finally, we must hold simultaneously, and in equal measure, the truths that 'I am filled with the Holy Spirit' and 'we are filled with the Holy Spirit'. To try and explain away one of these realities would be a

---

[412] R. Warren, Facebook, 9th November 2013,
https://www.facebook.com/pastorrickwarren/posts/10152036279630903,
retrieved 9th April 2014
[413] Galatians 5:22-23

mistake, and would require us to do origami with the texts. The fact of the matter is that each believer filled with the Holy Spirit shows an aspect of God which the next believer needs to see. There is a wonderful story about 'the Inklings', a literary group comprising C.S. Lewis, J.R.R. Tolkien, Charles Williams and several others. C.S. Lewis wrote once that when Charles Williams died, he believed that he would have more of Tolkien's attention and time, give that there was now one fewer member of the club. As it turned out, Lewis reports that he did not have more of Tolkien but less of him. Now that Charles was dead, he would never again see Tolkien's reaction to a specifically 'Charles' comment or quip. There was something about Charles that only he could bring out of Tolkien, which, now that he was dead, Lewis would never see again[414].

The point of relaying this story is that while I have the Spirit living inside of me personally, I need others around me to draw me out in particular ways, and likewise I need them. I cannot be fully who God made me to be, even though I am filled with the Spirit, unless I am in a context of others who strengthen me and whom I can strengthen. This is what it means to be filled with the Spirit; to be part of a family who are similarly filled with the Spirit.

---

[414] C. Duriez, 'Tolkien and C.S. Lewis: The Gift of Friendship', USA: Paulist Press, 2003, p80

# Nine

# The Spirit Creates, is Fully God and Makes Personal, Independent Decisions

## ✳✳✳

Now we come to the very heart of the issue. For many years, well-meaning Christians have not had a place for the Holy Spirit in their theology, and as such their search of the Scriptures hasn't included a grid for the Spirit, so He has been all but omitted. One of my theology lecturers once told a story of when he was a young Christian and attended a conference where he was confronted with a theological issue. The issue wasn't in the content of the teaching, but rather in the lyrics of a particular song which contained three similar verses. The first verse began "we praise you Father", the second began "we praise you Jesus" and the third "we praise you Spirit". My lecturer refused to sing this third verse, because at the time he didn't believe that the Spirit was God and therefore wasn't comfortable worshipping the Spirit in the same category as Jesus and the Father. I should say that he later changed his perspective, but I don't believe he was alone in his original belief. Is the Spirit to be viewed as equal to the Father and Jesus? Is He fully God in the same manner as the other two are? Is the trinity hierarchical in nature and, if so, where does the Spirit sit in this hierarchy? Should we worship the Spirit at all, or is He a force or agent of God rather than a fully divine person in his own right?

### The Spirit is a creator

Something that baffles me about the lack of theological books regarding the Holy Spirit is how frequently He is mentioned in the

Bible. I don't understand this lack of a correlation. The Spirit is mentioned more than 'idolatry', 'messiah' and 'leader' put together, and yet we have so many more books available on these subjects than about what the Bible says about the Holy Spirit. In the second verse of the opening chapter of the Bible, we read about the Spirit being involved in the creation process. While the earth was 'void' and before the earth had any form, the Spirit hovered over the surface of the waters[415]. This is not the place to debate creation and evolution, although I do hope to address this in a future book, but what we can see for our purposes is that the Spirit existed before anything was created. This makes the Spirit eternal, an attribute usually only ascribed to God himself[416]. The word which is used for 'hovered' is 'rachaph', which is used elsewhere of an eagle fluttering over her young[417], and of a holy quaking before the LORD[418]. These denote a significantly more pro-active rendering of the word than simply using 'moved', as they convey both the tenderness of a mother bird for her chicks as well as the power to make a person's bones quake. This verse shows us both that the Spirit was involved in creating the world, and gives us a glimpse of what the Spirit is like; tender yet powerful.

A phrase in Nehemiah 9 shows us the creative nature and power of the Spirit. We have already considered in chapter 5 how the Spirit instructs God's people, about which Nehemiah 9:20 is certainly talking, but this verse also speaks about the manna and water sent from heaven. This verse infers that the Spirit was involved in bringing about this miraculous provision of sustenance, which involved the creation of 'manna', a mysterious substance resembling wafers filled with honey. This was certainly a creative miracle, done by the hand of the Holy Spirit.

---

[415] Genesis 1:2
[416] Deuteronomy 33:27, Romans 16:26, etc.
[417] Deuteronomy 32:11
[418] Jeremiah 23:9

My favourite Old Testament book is Job because of its honest portrayal of human suffering as holding hands with the mysteries of God. When one of Job's 'friends', Elihu, is rebuking him, he utters the throw-away line, "The Spirit of God has made me, and the breath of the Almighty gives me life"[419]. As we discussed in chapter 6, much of the wisdom literature in the Bible takes the form of mirrored couplets, and Job is no exception. The first part of Elihu's phrase talks about the Spirit creating him, and presumably he would include all of humanity in that. The second part of the phrase echoes the first, but speaks of the Spirit as 'the breath of the Almighty'. The Hebrew words here for 'Spirit' and 'breath' are different, but they both convey the same connotations. The word for 'breath' has more life-giving qualities, but the words for 'spirit', 'breath' and 'wind' are used interchangeably in both the Old and New Testaments because of their similarities. That notwithstanding, Job affirms that the Spirit is involved in the creation of us as people.

The first chapter of Matthew shows us that the conception of Jesus was a miraculously creative event by the Holy Spirit. Matthew tells us that before Mary and Joseph slept together, Mary was found to be with child "from the Holy Spirit"[420]. When Joseph was visited by the angel to allay his fears, the angel uses the same phrase, telling him that what is conceived in her "is from the Holy Spirit"[421]. This shows us several things; firstly that Jesus' conception was of divine origin in a unique way. No other person's conception in Scripture is described in the manner that Jesus' conception is. Others, such as John the Baptist, show us that a child can be filled with the Spirit from their mother's womb, but only Jesus was, and ever will, be conceived 'from the Holy Spirit'. This is the method the triune God chose for the Second Person of the Trinity to become human; by the Holy Spirit. Jesus was fully human, which he got from Mary, but in his humanity

---

[419] Job 33:4
[420] Matthew 1:18
[421] Matthew 1:20

he was also fully divine; divinity that was combined with Mary's DNA by the Spirit. This was a creative miracle.

On a final note concerning the Spirit being involved in creation, we read in 2 Corinthians 3 of the Spirit bringing about the new covenant. Paul contrasts this with the old covenant, which he says is 'of the letter', which kills, but the new covenant is of the Spirit, which brings life[422]. Paul is clearly writing here of the nature of the covenants, one deadly and the other bringing life, but from what we know about the new covenant from elsewhere in Scripture, this covenant of the Spirit doesn't just 'bring life' in a theoretical way, but literally and actually *creates* new life in those who believe it. Paul may be echoing Jesus' words from John 6, where He says that the Spirit gives life but the flesh is no help at all[423]. There is an internal, personal and supernatural creative happening in the heart of one who believes in the covenant secured by Jesus' blood.

### The Spirit is personal

One of the attributes of God which is especially important in Christianity is that God is personal. As such, someone who is personal is responsible for making their own decisions. We see this as a character trait of the Holy Spirit, where Scripture describes Him as deciding to do certain things, such as choosing where to be or not to be. 1 Samuel 16 tells us that after the Spirit begins 'rushing upon' David on a regular basis, the Spirit decides to depart from Saul[424]. This shows us that the Spirit isn't merely a force at the whim of God, but rather that He makes decisions which seem fitting to Him, and which further the purposes of the triune God.

Isaiah asks the wonderfully rhetorical question, "Who can measure the Spirit of the LORD, and what man shows Him his counsel...?[425]"

---

[422] 2 Corinthians 3:6
[423] John 6:63
[424] 1 Samuel 16:13-14
[425] Isaiah 40:13

The more we ponder this question, the more ridiculous it becomes. The obvious and heavily implied answer is that 'no one can measure the Spirit'. This is partly because He is not material or finite, which are the requirements for something to be measured. The Hebrew word used here for 'measure', *'takan'*, has a broader application than simply using a tape measure to find the length of a room. Other renderings of this word include 'to regulate', 'to estimate', 'to be equal' or 'to test'. Therefore, this makes the foolishness of Isaiah's statement even greater. What is being questioned here is not simply the physical dimensions of an infinite, immaterial, eternal being, but rather the notion of bringing God down to our level to be subjected to our stipulations and criteria. Obviously this is folly, as is the idea that we could give Him counsel. Jesus refers to the Spirit as "the counsellor" in the King James translation of John 14:26, and while other translations opt for words such as 'helper', 'comforter' or 'advocate', the original Greek word certainly has the connotation of one who gives counsel. For a person to attempt to give counsel to the eternal Spirit of God is both arrogant and presumptuous. The Spirit counsels us, not the other way around.

Isaiah goes on to write more about the personal nature of the Spirit in chapter 63. While recounting the course of the relationship between the people of Israel and the LORD, Isaiah writes that "they rebelled and grieved his Holy Spirit"[426], the result of which was that God turned to be their enemy and fought against them. This is quickly mitigated by the next verse which says that God remembered the days of Moses and led His people again. The nature of how God is depicted in the Old Testament is a sizable topic, out-with the scope of this book[427]. However, for our purposes these verses tell us that the Spirit is personal and can also be grieved. If the Spirit is personal, this must mean that He has a personality, and as such is a person. If He is a person, this must mean He can be known in the

---

[426] Isaiah 63:10

[427] For further reading on this issue, see 'Is God a Moral Monster?' by Paul Copan

way that I know a friend, especially if, as we explored in the last chapter, He lives inside of me. Much of western theology and practise of late has focused on our relationship with Jesus, and I entirely agree that this should be upheld as one of the most important doctrines of the church. However, if we believe in a truly triune God comprising of three divine persons, it stands to reason that we could get to know them each in a personal way. A curious verse in Zechariah has the LORD saying that He has set His Spirit "at rest in the north country"[428]. A force or belief system does not achieve rest; only a living being rests, much like God does in the creation narrative in Genesis 2. This gives more weight to the argument that the Holy Spirit is some*one* to be known, not simply a force without a face. I believe we need to cultivate our relationships with the Holy Spirit individually, as well as corporately, as an expression of worship.

The untimely deaths of Ananias and Sapphira in Acts 5 also shed some light on the personal nature of the Holy Spirit. When Peter confronts Ananias about the true amount he sold his land for, Peter's problem doesn't seem to be with their keeping a part of the proceeds[429], but rather, Peter asks Ananias why "Satan filled your heart to lie to the Holy Spirit"[430], at which Ananias drops dead in front of them. The story is very similar with Sapphira, who is asked the same question, gives the same answer and receives the same fate. I don't believe that the money was the issue here, but rather that they conspired in their hearts to lie to the Spirit. This implies a breach of trust, which you can only have with a person, not a force. We should note that it is not stated in the passage, or elsewhere in the Bible, that the Spirit killed the couple. The short answer is that we don't know what caused their deaths; the text doesn't tell us. No steps are taken against a guilty human party, so it looks unlikely that it was a member of the church who killed them. Furthermore, it

---

[428] Zechariah 6:8
[429] Acts 5:4
[430] Acts 5:3

would be out of character with what we have seen of the Holy Spirit to say that He killed them, and while this is not impossible, it is improbable. Personally, I believe that the mention of Satan in this chapter in verse 3 is telling; I believe that Satan killed Ananias and Sapphira in an attempt to frighten the church. However, I recognise that there is disagreement about these events.

Acts gives us two further examples of the Spirit being personal. The first is in Acts 7, where, during the speech which ultimately ends in him being stoned to death, Stephen attacks the gathered crowd, including the high priest, by saying;

> "You stiff-necked people, uncircumcised in heart and ears, you always resist the Holy Spirit. As your fathers did, so do you"[431].

At this they picked up stones and killed him, but his assertion that they 'resist' the Holy Spirit goes beyond saying simply 'you didn't do as the law required'. Rather, they resisted the promptings of someone who was trying to get them to live and act in a righteous way. Later, in the Jerusalem council's letter to the brothers in Antioch, Syria and Cilicia, they write that instructions they give them weren't over burdensome, because "it seemed right to the Holy Spirit and to [them]"[432] not to make them so. This decision was made with the Holy Spirit, and the casual way in which it is reported gives the impression that the Spirit was in the room when the decision was made. Theologically, this is correct of course, but Luke reports this not as a theological truth but as an experiential reality; the Spirit was in the room as much as Paul and Barnabas were in the room, and was equally involved in the decision making.

Paul writes in Romans that when we are weak, that is, when the pressures of life oppress us to the point where we cannot pray, "the Spirit himself intercedes for us with groanings too deep for words."[433]

---

[431] Acts 7:51
[432] Acts 15:28

In this instance, looking at the original Greek sheds no light on the meaning of his word; the word for 'groaning' is only used in one other place in the New Testament, and is translated in exactly the same way. What this verse seem to be saying is that there is a method of praying which goes beyond words. I have a close friend who, on occasion, has experienced this 'groaning too deep for words' when he has been spending time in prayer. His explanation of this is the following;

> "The heart moves with joy, compassion, pain and honesty towards God, and He responds. In this cosmic yet personal interchange between creator and created, the body jolts with spasms that express my internal conditions better than any words could."

Although I have never experienced this myself, because of the mutual trust we share, I believe that he is really experiencing God in, what appears to be, an entirely Biblical manner. But notice how this is described in Romans 8; "the Spirit Himself intercedes for us..."[434] We should pay as much attention to who is bringing these experiences as to the experiences themselves. Paul's casual use of the pronoun 'himself' to refer to the Spirit shows us the personal nature of the Spirit, and that He is ready and willing to help us when we need Him. In the very next verse, Paul elaborates on this idea, saying that he who searches hearts knows the mind of the Spirit, because the Spirit intercedes for the saints according to the will of God[435]. He who searches the hearts is, in all likelihood, God Himself, as is referred to in several passages such as 1 Samuel 16:7, which says that while man looks at the outward appearance, God looks at the heart[436]. Furthermore, Luke 16:15 explains that while we might seek to justify ourselves before men, God knows our hearts. The

---

[433] Romans 8:26
[434] Romans 8:16
[435] Romans 8:27
[436] See also; 1 Chronicles 28:9, Proverbs 15:11, 17:3, Jeremiah 11:20, 17:10, and 1 Thessalonians 2:4

Spirit meets us in our weakness and intercedes on our behalf according to God's will.

Three final Scriptures describe the Spirit in very personal terms; those being that He can be grieved, quenched and outraged. Ephesians 4 has Paul urging the church to not grieve the Holy Spirit of God. The most frequent usage of this word rendered here as 'grieve' is 'to make sorrowful', such as we read of the rich young man's reaction to Jesus telling him to sell all he has in Matthew 19. This shows us that the Spirit can be made to be sorrowful; this is not the way you would describe a 'force' or the will of someone else. The context of this verse in Ephesians 4 is Paul urging the church to live in harmony with one another; not to let anger, slander, lies or theft be in their midst. This is how to make the Spirit sorrowful; by nursing a grudge, saying hurtful or untrue things and by stealing others property or dignity[437]. It would not be hard to see how a person could be upset by these things, and the Spirit is a person who has sealed the saints for the day of redemption and therefore is connected to those whom He has sealed. To offend or injure a saint is to grieve the Spirit.

In Paul's first letter to the Thessalonian church, Paul bids them farewell with a series of instructions to them. One of which is:

> "Do not quench the Spirit. Do not despise prophecies, but test everything; hold fast what is good"[438].

I believe that this is one of the most important verses in the Bible, and is the very essence of an Incessant Theology. This verse firstly tells us not to quench the Spirit. To quench something means, 'to extinguish', 'to go out', 'to suppress' or 'to stifle'. There are certain sections of the Christian church that hold to the notion that God's purposes cannot be quenched or extinguished by our actions. While I agree that we cannot add anything to our salvation, it does not

---

[437] Ephesians 4:25-32
[438] 1 Thessalonians 5:19-20

stand to reason that we have no influence on anything in the Christian life. We *can* quench the Spirit, or else why would Paul have told the Thessalonians not to? Because He is personal, He can be snubbed and made redundant to bring about what God would say to us through prophesy. It seems reasonable to assert that the ways, or at least some of the ways, we can quench the Spirit is to despise prophecies, or else to not test prophecies. Another way to read this verse is; "Do not think that prophecies have nothing to offer, but always test and scrutinise them to assert whether they are genuine or not." We can fall into two equally fatal traps; the first is to despise prophesy and either never allow it to happen or else to ignore and ridicule it when it does. The second fatal approach is to believe and act like everything said under the guise of 'prophesy' is Divine truth, when this would be equally unbiblical and unwise. Paul's solution to this tension is to tell the Thessalonians not to despise prophecies, but equally to test everything and hold fast only to what is good.

Finally, the writer to the Hebrews informs his readers that if they are not in the covenant of Grace, they might as well have trampled Christ under their feet, have profaned the blood of the covenant and have outraged the Spirit of Grace[439]. While it is probably the case that the writer was using hyperbole here to make the point that if you are outside of the covenant with Christ you have no help anywhere else, he has no trouble in personifying the Spirit by saying that He can be 'outraged', or 'insulted'. It would be good to remember at this point that this is the Spirit whose fruit includes joy, and it would be untrue and unfair to paint Him as moody. However, because He is personal, He has feelings which can be hurt, grieved or insulted. As such, we should avoid doing what Paul in Ephesians 4 and 1 Thessalonians 5, as well as the writer to the Hebrews in chapter 10, says can hinder the Spirit's relationship with us. Just like in any relationship, we are responsible for half of the upkeep of the friendship we share with the Holy Spirit. He is God and we are not, but He is a personal God like we are personal creatures.

---

[439] Hebrews 10:26-29

## The Spirit is fully God

Throughout the preceding chapters I have repeatedly referred to the Spirit as being fully God. I have done so because I believe this to be true with all my heart, but up until now I have yet to explain why this is so. To this question we now turn; where does the Christian faith get its basis for believing that the Holy Spirit is fully God in the same way that Jesus and the Father are each fully God?

Of the twelve biblical references to the divinity of the Spirit, half of them come from the Gospels and the other half from the epistles. One of the primary reasons that the Spirit is believed to be God by the overwhelming majority of Christian traditions is because of how Jesus speaks of Him in the Gospels. In all of the synoptic gospels, Jesus warns about blasphemy against the Holy Spirit. This is an interesting phrase, and we will discuss exactly what it means in a moment, but we would be unwise to overlook the obvious statement being made about the nature of the Holy Spirit here; if He can be blasphemed against, this means that He is God. The very definition of 'blasphemy' is to slander God or to speak ill of divine majesty. Jesus speaks of the Holy Spirit with reverence, holding Him to be divine in the same way as He Himself is divine.

> "Therefore I tell you, every sin and blasphemy will be forgiven people, but the blasphemy against the Spirit will not be forgiven. And whoever speaks a word against the Son of Man will be forgiven, but whoever speaks against the Holy Spirit will not be forgiven, either in this age or in the age to come"[440].

This is very telling, as it reveals the importance with which Jesus regards the Holy Spirit. Astoundingly, Jesus claims that blasphemy against Himself will be forgiven, but blasphemy against the Holy Spirit will not be forgiven[441]. These can be quite frightening Scriptures, but I don't believe they need be, for three reasons.

---

[440] Matthew 12:31-32

Firstly, because the Spirit convicts people of sin, which we will explore in the next chapter, if we blaspheme against Him, we damage our relationship with Him to the point where our consciences are shut off to His voice and promptings. The result of this is that we will be unable to be repent of sin and so can become consumed by it. Perhaps this is what Paul was referring to in 1 Timothy 1 when he wrote;

> "...holding faith and a good conscience. By rejecting this, some have made shipwreck of their faith, among whom are Hymenaeus and Alexander, whom I have handed over to Satan that they may learn not to blaspheme"[442].

Of course, there is much disagreement about these verses, but I believe that this interpretation is in keeping with other accepted Christian doctrines about the atonement and the nature of sin.

The second reason I believe that Christians needn't worry these verses is the very fact that they are worrying about them. I once heard a helpful phrase about this, which said that if you are worried about whether you've committed the unforgivable sin, you can be sure that you haven't committed it. Blaspheming against the Holy Spirit would result in an inability to feel guilt about blaspheming against the Holy Spirit. I find this perspective helpful.

The third and final reason why believers needn't fear blaspheming against the Holy Spirit is because those who are blaspheming will almost certainly know about it. The God I worship is a Father whose arms are open wide to all who would come to Him; He is watching for the prodigal coming home along the road and runs towards him when He sees him. He does not turn people away on a technicality; sin that is unintentional and/or unknown was provided for in the Old Testament sacrificial system[443], and therefore was paid for in full at

---

[441] Mark 3:29, Luke 12:10
[442] 1 Timothy 1:19-20
[443] Leviticus 4:2-27, Numbers 15:22-29

the cross[444]. However, those who blaspheme are usually aware of it. If one consciously blasphemes against the Holy Spirit, that is, to bring His name or activity into disrepute, I believe that all but the most immature believers will know what they are doing. One of the so-called 'ten commandments' contains the instruction to "not take the name of the LORD your God in vain."[445] 'In vain' means to consider something as empty, false, worthless or as nothing, and this is the result of blasphemy; to render the things of God as of no worth or presenting them as false. For every wonderful story of the Spirit meeting someone in a time of need, or bringing healing, or seeing someone give their life to Christ, there are stories of people exploiting the name of the Holy Spirit for their own gain. These include prosperity gospel preachers, whose doctrine says that those who are suffering are suffering because of their lack of faith, or that people need to 'give until it hurts' to get God to bless them. These thoughts are not only destructive to the fabric of the human spirit, but they also bring the Holy Spirit into disrepute. There is an old adage which claims that we are the only Bible that many people will ever read. This is true with people's doctrine of the Holy Spirit; those who use the name of the Spirit to propagate an all-purpose lying mechanism will have to answer for themselves, as well for those they have led astray.

The true way to worship God is by the Spirit. Jesus says so in John's gospel, where He explains to the Samaritan woman that in the reign of the messiah there wouldn't be a geographical place where people would need to go to worship God, but that God's people would worship 'in Spirit and in truth'. In the same verse, Jesus says that 'God is Spirit', which probably refers to His immateriality, but it would be strange to use the word 'spirit' and not refer to the third person of the Trinity[446].

---

[444] Hebrews 9:7, 13-14
[445] Exodus 20:7
[446] John 4:23-24

At the very end of Matthew's gospel, Jesus is explaining to the disciples what they are to do after he ascends into heaven.

> "Go therefore and make disciples of all nations, baptizing them in the name of the Father and of the Son and of the Holy Spirit."[447]

Just as it is Jesus who affirms that the Spirit is God because He can be blasphemed against, it is Jesus who affirms that the Spirit is God in equality with the Father and the Son. If there was any doubt that the Spirit was God, Jesus removes it with this statement. Notice also that there are hints of the Trinity here; Jesus instructs the disciples to baptize people into the 'name' of the Father, Son and Spirit; one name for three persons.

The apostle Paul picks up the argument for the Spirit's divinity throughout his epistles. He makes a curious statement in Romans 8 about the Spirit, which is also pleasantly Trinitarian;

> "If the Spirit of Him who raised Jesus from the dead dwells in you, he who raised Christ Jesus from the dead will also give life to your mortal bodies through his Spirit who dwells in you."[448]

If we look at this verse in detail, it yields some very interesting information. Firstly, the phrase "if the Spirit of Him who raised Jesus from the dead dwells in you" tells us that the Spirit who dwells in us is the Spirit of God, because it was the Spirit of God who raised Christ from the dead. This is because God dwells in us by his Spirit, as we explored in the previous chapter. Secondly, this verse tells us that because it was the Spirit who raised Jesus from death, it follows that the Spirit is God, because we read in Acts that it was God who raised Jesus from death[449]. Ergo, through the piecing together of

---

[447] Matthew 28:19
[448] Romans 8:11
[449] Acts 2:24, 4:10

several verses, we see here that Paul is affirming the divinity of the Holy Spirit.

Three verses in 1 Corinthians also lead us to this conclusion. Firstly, when Paul writes that no one can comprehend the thoughts of God except the Spirit of God[450]. This verse points to the equality of the Spirit with God, citing that no one knows a person's thoughts except the spirit of that person. If we keep in mind the verses from Isaiah which tells us that God's ways and thoughts are higher than our ways and thoughts[451], we see that for someone to comprehend the thoughts of God must be equal to Him. Paul tells us here that the Spirit comprehends the thoughts of God, and so we can safely conclude that the Spirit is equal to God.

Paul continues this line of thought a few verses later by explaining that the natural person doesn't accept the things of the Spirit of God, because he considers them foolish[452]. There is an uncomfortable truth in this statement, because Christianity has historically been very poor at recognising the things of the Spirit of God. While I believe Paul is writing about those who do not trust in Jesus for their salvation, there is an application for the church. If when God 'moves' our response is to cling to the previous way we have 'done church' instead of making room for the Spirit to move and work, we are treating the things of the Spirit as folly. This is essentially to say that we know better than the Spirit of God, which is an unwise statement to make.

As I write this, I can imagine the responses of some of the more conservative Christians I know. These Christians may well be thinking, 'we have trusted the Spirit throughout the history of the church, and our current church practise is based on the Bible'. To this I would applaud and agree with what they are saying, but I would add that there have been many Christians who, over the

---

[450] 1 Corinthians 2:11
[451] Isaiah 55:9
[452] 1 Corinthians 2:14

years, have undertaken to follow the Bible for instructions about how to be the church. I believe that it is a part of human nature to want to be correct. In light of this, it would be fair to say that those who interpreted the Bible 700 years ago wanted to be correct also, and I believe that they thought their interpretation was the correct one. So how can both of these things be true? How can scholars reading the same texts 700 years apart come to such vastly different conclusions? The answer, I believe, is that the Sprit illuminates different parts of Scripture at different times. Martin Luther, for example, was transformed by his reading about justification by faith in Romans, but had little or no regard for the gifts of the Spirit. However, the same Scriptures were read in the 20th century and people came to the conclusion that the gifts are for the contemporary church. We cannot cling blindly to the ways of the past by appealing to an historic move of the Spirit; the Spirit is fully God and is therefore eternal, and as such wishes to meet, move and motivate today's church today.

We have already made reference to the church and the believer being the temple of God, and that God dwells in us by His Spirit. The phrasing of this in 1 Corinthians 3 tells us something about the deity of the Spirit. "Do you not know that you are God's temple and that God's Spirit dwells in you?"[453] If we look at this verse using algebra, we learn something.

> "Do you not know that you are X's temple and that X's Spirit lives in you?"

Obviously, X equals 'God', and so if we are God's temple, we can also say that the Spirit is God's Spirit. We see a further affirmation of the Spirit's deity in 2 Corinthians 3, where Paul writes that "the Lord is the Spirit, and where the Spirit of the Lord is, there is freedom ... For this comes from the Lord who is the Spirit."[454]

---

[453] 1 Corinthians 3:16
[454] 2 Corinthians 3:17-18

This is a popular verse, and understandably so. This verse unequivocally declares that the Lord is the Spirit, and His presence brings freedom. However, the phrasing of this verse isn't the strictest possible translation, and the original Greek could equally, or even more easily, be rendered as "Now the Spirit is the LORD"[455]. In fact, this is how the Wycliffe Bible translation of the New Testament renders it. While both translations are legitimate, one *implies* that the Spirit is the Lord while the other says it more explicitly.

Lastly, when the writer of the book of Hebrews is explaining Christ's role as high priest, he writes that Christ offered himself to God without blemish, He did so "through the eternal Spirit"[456]. The eternality of the Spirit is intrinsic in His being God, and as such could play a part in the atonement. Being eternal means to be without beginning and without end; who other than God could be described in such terms?

**Conclusions**

In light of these findings, there are several responses we should make. As we have journeyed through the Scriptures over this chapter, and the previous chapters, I would hope that our ideas about the Holy Spirit have been challenged and perhaps even changed. In light of what we've seen of the divinity of the Spirit in this chapter, I propose two responses.

Firstly, we should esteem the Spirit as fully God in all of our theological dealings. This means we should look to Him and His eternal wisdom when making decisions of conscience, church protocol or personal growth. This also means we should stop speaking about the Spirit in a manner which is unworthy of the LORD God Almighty; our sermons, worship and prayers as well as our blogs, books and tweets should give the Spirit the glory which is due

---

[455] W. Grudem, Systematic Theology, Nottingham: Inter Varsity Press, 2007, p233
[456] Hebrews 9:14

to Him, and not in a superficial, lip-service kind of way but in a manner which expresses something of our heart's cry. After all, the Spirit lives inside of us. An example of esteeming the Spirit in this way is with regard to creation. Genesis 1, 2 and 3 mention all three persons of the Trinity, but as this chapter has shown us, the Spirit continues to create new life, both physically and spiritually.

The second way we can honour the divinity of the Spirit is to address and connect with Him personally. Jesus refers to the Spirit as the 'helper' or 'counsellor', and such a person is, by definition, a personal character. I have been intentional in my references to the Spirit as 'He' as opposed to 'it' or even 'he', because I would refer to the Father and Jesus using the capitalized personal pronoun, and while grammatical customs can be argued until kingdom come, they do denote something about where we place our emphasis. The Spirit is 'He' for two reasons; firstly He is a *person* of the Trinity, and secondly Jesus refers to Him as such.

Because the Spirit is a personal, creator God, and is equal in deity with the Father and the Son, we can trust in Him and rely on Him when the Bible says that He lives within us. He is not a force, not even a force for good; He is a person, and a person with a remit. We will now turn to the role of the Spirit in conviction, conversion and building up the church.

# Ten

# The Spirit Convicts, Converts and Strengthens the Church

## ✱✱✱

When I was studying theology at the International Christian College in Glasgow, I was a very contented young man. However, there seemed to be some omissions in the syllabus with regards to the Holy Spirit, so when the time came in my final year to write a dissertation, I chose to write about the link between the Spirit and conversion within protestant churches in Glasgow. By writing to every protestant church I could acquire details for, totalling more than 170, I statistically proved that churches which experience regular demonstrations of the gifts of the Spirit saw three times as many conversions as churches which never see the gifts demonstrated[457].

This is a bold claim, and while I can back this up with numerical evidence, the question remains, 'is this a Biblical idea?' Does the Holy Spirit bring about conversion, and, for that matter, conviction? And does He also build up the church? These are the questions we will be exploring in this chapter.

While in some ways it should not be surprising that there are no verses about the Spirit convicting or converting people in the Old Testament, I was still a little taken aback when I realised this. I believe that one reason for this is that the way we understand religious conversion today is very different from how a person would become a member of the nation of Israel in the Old Testament, in

---

[457] For a more detailed explanation of my research, see Appendix 1, page 203

that while 'conversions' as we would understand them did happen, these were both rare and were more holistic in nature. Allow me to explain; today, when we think of someone being 'converted to Christianity', we probably mean a change of heart which leads to a change of action, in response to hearing the gospel. In the old covenant, this was a much more of a practical event, where the person, their family, their land, animals and possessions would join a community as well as a religion. They would be joining a theocratic society, and a part of that would mean a change of heart inclined towards the LORD. For some reason, the Spirit isn't recorded as being involved in conversion in the Old Testament, and so it is to the New Testament we turn in order to see the Spirit convicting and converting people.

## The Spirit convicts and converts

Somewhat more astonishing than the lack of mention of the Spirit's converting remit in the Old Testament is how little of it we find in the Gospels. This is perhaps because a lot of what we find in the Gospels is Jesus 'preparing the way', as John the Baptist puts it, for what would ultimately happen at the cross and through Christ's resurrection. It is not until we get to Acts and the epistles that the true extent of what Christ did is explained. That said, there are two references to the Spirit with regards to conversion in the Gospel of John, both in chapter 3.

> "Jesus answered, "Truly, truly, I say to you, unless one is born of water and the Spirit, he cannot enter the kingdom of God. That which is born of the flesh is flesh, and that which is born of the Spirit is spirit. Do not marvel that I said to you, 'You must be born again.' The wind blows where it wishes, and you hear its sound, but you do not know where it comes from or where it goes. So it is with everyone who is born of the Spirit"[458].

---

[458] John 3:5-8

This is a part of Jesus' conversation with Nicodemus, from where we get one of the most famous verses in the Bible. Nicodemus was a teacher of Israel, clearly a learned man, and yet he came to Jesus at night to quiz him about the things of heaven. I have always assumed that he came to Jesus at night because he was uncomfortable about being seen with Jesus in daylight, and his line of questioning seems to give this impression. Nicodemus is a seeker, and Jesus responds to him on an appropriate level. Nicodemus is initially confused about the term 'being born again', wrongly taking it literally, but Jesus' statement in verse 5 clarifies that He is in fact talking about something spiritual. Interestingly, Jesus includes in this statement an element of being in communion with God that had never been uttered before; 'you must be born of water and the Spirit'.

There have been many centuries of discussion about these verses, but Jesus seems to be speaking about repentance and regeneration. Repentance leads to baptism, described as 'being born of water', and being regenerated is the work of the Spirit, as we will see throughout this chapter. In other words, Jesus is laying out the path by which people can come to God in His Kingdom; water and Spirit. Jesus then goes on to describe the nature of the Spirit and, I believe, the heavenly realms. He uses the analogy of the wind as an example of something that is, to first century eyes, unpredictable, asserting that this is the style of the Spirit; He cannot be controlled or contained, He is unpredictable and He is powerful. Much later, Titus would affirm that the Spirit is involved in both regeneration and renewal at the start of a believer's journey[459].

This pattern of repentance and baptism followed by the coming of the Holy Spirit is repeated in Acts. When the gathered crowd had heard Peter give his sermon explaining the events of Pentecost and that they were the ones responsible for crucifying the Messiah, they are devastated and beseech him, saying "what should we do?"[460]

---

[459] Titus 3:5
[460] Acts 2:37

Peter's response is to tell them to repent and be baptized for the forgiveness of their sins, and that they will then receive the gift of the Holy Spirit[461]. While there is not an explicit mention of the Spirit bringing conversion here, He is strongly implicated as a part of the whole package of coming to Christ.

Later on, when Peter is in the house of a gentile named Cornelius, he is in the middle of giving a sermon about who Jesus is and what He had done, including the resurrection and His fulfilment of the prophecies about Him, when "the Holy Spirit fell on all who heard the word"[462]. Peter's Jewish companions who witnessed this were astonished at the lack of distinction the Spirit made between Jew and gentile, because those gathered were speaking in tongues and praising God. Peter wisely concludes that the only reasonable response to these events is to baptise them in the name of Jesus, showing no partiality because the Spirit shows no partiality. Interestingly, the pattern which we saw in John 3 and Acts 2 of people encountering water *before* encountering the Holy Spirit is reversed in this passage. Here, the gathered people encounter the Holy Spirit before, or at least simultaneously with, being converted. As such, we should not be too prescriptive in our theology of conversion. Like those in Cornelius' house, it may be that people meet the Holy Spirit in a meaningful way before they formally and 'officially' give their lives to Christ.

In Romans, Paul makes several references to the Spirit bringing about conversion. The first of these is found in Romans 2, where he is explaining the connection between 'being Jewish' and being 'in Christ'. Paul writes;

> "For no one is a Jew who is merely one outwardly, nor is circumcision outward and physical. But a Jew is one inwardly, and circumcision is a matter of the heart, by the Spirit, not by the letter"[463].

---

[461] Acts 2:38
[462] Acts 10:44

What Paul is amazingly saying here to those of his readers who were Jewish is that their 'Jewishness' is not a physical, outward sign, but rather true Jewishness is a matter of the heart, by the Spirit[464]. Being truly in a covenant with God is not a matter of outward physical features, but rather of inward spiritual ones.

Paul continues this manner of writing in 2 Corinthians 3, where he compares the old covenant "of death, carved in letters on stone"[465] with the new covenant of the Spirit. He says that the ministry of the former came with such glory that the Israelites couldn't even look at Moses' face[466], but that this was the ministry of condemnation[467]. In contrast, the ministry of the Spirit is even more glorious, because His ministry is of righteousness[468] and is permanent, whereas the former ministry has passed away[469]. The Spirit is the ministry of righteousness; making unholy sinners become holy saints before God. Paul later explains that this same Spirit, who is the Lord, transforms us from one degree of glory to another[470], showing the on-going sanctification of the Spirit after we've been regenerated by Him.

In Romans 8, Paul explains that we have been set free from the law of sin and death by "the law of the Spirit of life"[471]. It would not be a stretch to assert that this is a reference to conversion, given that the Spirit is said to have freed us from the law of sin and death 'in Christ Jesus'; a potent metaphor for salvation. Paul expands on this a few verses later when he describes the body as being dead because of sin, but the Spirit is life because of righteousness. This is in the

---

[463] Romans 2:28-29
[464] Romans 2:29
[465] 2 Corinthians 3:7
[466] 2 Corinthians 3:7
[467] 2 Corinthians 3:9
[468] 2 Corinthians 3:9
[469] 2 Corinthians 3:11
[470] 2 Corinthians 3:18
[471] Romans 8:2

context of discussing the Spirit living inside the believer; the body has been crucified with Christ but the Spirit is alive, and as such the believer is alive. Again, the righteousness being discussed here, by which the Spirit brings life, is the righteousness of Christ.

The Spirit is involved in sanctification as well as justification; Romans 15 tells us that Paul was ministering to the gentiles so that their offering "may be acceptable, sanctified by the Holy Spirit"[472]. Paul was concerned that the gentiles' worship be acceptable, and would be made holy by the ministry of the Spirit. This thread is picked up in 1 Corinthians 6, where Paul tells the Corinthians that they were washed and sanctified and justified in the name of Jesus and by the Spirit of our God[473]. In some traditional Christian thinking about salvation, the redemption purchased on our behalf was done by Christ, and the Spirit is often relegated to a sub-clause of this or else omitted all together. However, this verse cuts right across that thinking; while it is certainly true that Christ's death and resurrection was the *mechanism* by which salvation was attained, without the ministry of the Spirit to apply it to me, there is a missing link in the chain, and the salvation bought with Jesus' blood is rendered ineffective. The Spirit is not just a footnote in salvation history; He is essential for salvation. The disciple John adds baptism to this equation, saying that the Spirit and the blood and the water all agree.[474]

Peter elaborates on this thought in his first letter, writing to the "elect exiles... in the sanctification of the Spirit for obedience to Jesus Christ and for sprinkling in his blood"[475]. This explains that the Spirit sanctifies us in order to increase our obedience to Christ Jesus, and for the initial application of His blood to our lives. In 2 Thessalonians Paul writes something very similar, explaining that we are sanctified by the Spirit to believe in the truth[476].

---

[472] Romans 15:16
[473] 1 Corinthians 6:11
[474] 1 John 5:8
[475] 1 Peter 1:2

The Spirit is also the *sign* of salvation, for it is only by the Spirit that anyone can say "Jesus is Lord"[477]. Equally, nobody speaking by the Spirit will ever say "Jesus be accursed". This duality of this statement is wonderfully helpful in our quest to understand the nature of the Holy Spirit. Firstly, it tells us that the Spirit is the one who enables people to say 'Jesus is Lord'. Declaring this is the very definition of what being a Christian is about. Secondly, it gives us a safeguard as to those claiming to be speaking by the Spirit, but about whom we have our doubts. If such a person declares 'Jesus be accursed', either explicitly or implicitly, Paul is assuring us that this person is not speaking by the Spirit, and as such should not be listened to. Of course, it is possible that someone could avoid saying this exact phrase, but be speaking in a manner which implies that Jesus is accursed; such a person should be corrected and not heeded. John's first letter gives a similar test; writing against the emerging gnostic theology[478], John instructs his readers that they will know the Spirit of God because the Spirit of God causes people to confess that Jesus has come in the flesh[479]. Just like someone who proclaimed that Jesus is accursed, someone who denies the humanity of Christ should equally not be listened to. This is not to say that such a person should be excommunicated or shunned, but there is a place for drawing a line in the sand and insisting that there are certain key truths about which we cannot compromise.

In his second letter to the Corinthian church, Paul asks whether he would need a letter of recommendation to them or from them. He answers his own question by saying that the church themselves is his letter of recommendation, written on their hearts for all to see. This letter is written with "the Spirit of the living God"[480]; a clear

---

[476] 2 Thessalonians 2:13
[477] 1 Corinthians 12:3
[478] Gnostic Christians in the 1st, 2nd and 3rd centuries held to the belief that the spiritual side of the world was good while the physical side was bad. In light of this, they denied that Jesus had actually become flesh as they believed that this would pollute His spirit.
[479] 1 John 4:2

metaphor for the Spirit convicting the church and bringing them to maturity. Paul saw his letter of recommendation in the hearts and lives of the members of this church, one which was written by the Spirit.

In Galatians, Paul asks an almost rhetorical question; "Having begun by the Spirit, are you now being perfected by the flesh?"[481] The question has an almost ridiculous tone to it; not only is it not beneficial, it's not even possible to do it. This does, however, affirm what we have seen time and again; the Galatian church began by the Spirit. As conversion is the beginning of the Christian life, Paul is saying here that conversion is the work of the Spirit. Paul affirms this later on in Galatians, where he uses the example of Sarah and Hagar to make the point that people who are 'born according to the Spirit' are being persecuted by people "born according to the flesh"[482]. Being 'born according to the Spirit' has echoes of Jesus' conversation with Nicodemus, adding more weight to the belief that the Spirit brings about conversion.

Paul's opening lines to the Thessalonian church put a different spin on our understanding of the gospel. He writes that they are brothers loved by God, because the gospel came to them "not only in word, but also in power and in the Holy Spirit and with full conviction"[483]. This three-way implementation of the gospel should be noted. The gospel certainly *is* words, in that it is the *message* of salvation, but it is also a matter of power and of the Holy Spirit. It is interesting that 'power', 'words' and 'the Holy Spirit' are mentioned separately, because many Christians can make the mistake of collating 'the Holy Spirit' with either 'power' or 'words', thereby effectively ignoring one aspect of His ministry. If we assume that the Holy Spirit acts only through words, that is by the preaching of the gospel, then we will absorb 'power' into the ministry of the Holy Spirit through preaching.

---

[480] 2 Corinthians 3:3
[481] Galatians 3:3
[482] Galatians 4:29
[483] 1 Thessalonians 1:5

Equally, if we assume that the Spirit acts only through power, that is through miracles and signs and wonders, then we will neglect the aspect of His remit that works through preaching. What Paul is saying in this verse is that the gospel comes to people by words and power and by the Holy Spirit; the combination of which brings full conviction.

## The Spirit Strengthens the Church

Thus far we have extensively considered the Spirit's role in convicting and converting. However, Scripture also tells us that the Spirit has a part to play in bringing unity within the church and in building her up, as well as in adding people to the church. Paul's letters to the Corinthians and the Ephesians are particularly helpful on this topic.

In his famous chapter about the gifts of the Spirit in 1 Corinthians 12, Paul is at pains to urge the church not to divide into factions over the variety of gifts. He explains that there are many gifts, but one Spirit who gives them all[484], before deconstructing racial and social divisions too;

> "For in one Spirit we were all baptised into one body—Jews or Greeks, slaves or free—and all were made to drink of one Spirit"[485].

Notice the frequency of the word 'one' in this single sentence. Paul is definite that there is one Spirit and one body which we were all baptised into, regardless of race, social status or gifting. The Spirit is one and so the body is one.

Paul adds to this imperative of oneness a few chapters later, when he implores the Corinthians to use the manifestations of the Spirit, for which they are so eager, in order to build up the church. Actually,

---

[484] 1 Corinthians 12:11
[485] 1 Corinthians 12:13

Paul goes beyond suggesting this as a good idea, instead telling them to "strive to excel in building up the church"[486]. Essentially, he is saying that in the midst of their enthusiasm for manifestations of the Spirit, they must never let slip from their minds the importance of doing so to encourage those in the church. This would exclude the idea of using manifestations in order to build up one's own ego, to promote one gifting over another or using them to tear down someone else. The manifestations of the Spirit must, this passage tells us, be used to build up the whole church.

Paul's final canonical words to the Corinthian church are often used at the end of certain types of services as a mantra to be recited. Interestingly, this is one of the few verses in Scripture which explicitly mentions all three persons of the Trinity in the same sentence;

> "The grace of the Lord Jesus Christ and the love of God and the fellowship of the Holy Spirit be with you all"[487].

According to this verse, the Lord Jesus Christ brings grace, God brings love and the Holy Spirit brings fellowship. Of course, one of the purposes of studying theology is to gather everything that Scripture says about a given topic. So, this verse saying that Jesus brings grace and the Spirit brings fellowship does not mean to say that the Spirit never brings grace; we've already seen how the Spirit applies grace to our lives. I don't believe that this verse is making definitive statements about the specific roles of the persons of the Trinity. However, it is curious to notice that the role of bringing fellowship to the believers is ascribed to the Holy Spirit. The original word used for 'fellowship' is 'koinōnia', which has a very intimate connotation. This is the kind of connection the Spirit brings to the church; intimacy.

---

486 1 Corinthians 14:12
487 2 Corinthians 13:14

In the seemingly unending canonical discussion concerning being circumcised or not, and the implications grace has for the law, Paul makes an extensive appeal in Ephesians 2 for Jews and gentiles to put aside their differences and to be one in Christ in light of the work of the cross. Paul explains that through Christ, both Jew and gentile have access "in one Spirit to the Father"[488]. The dividing line between Jews and gentiles is done away with for those who are in Christ, and one result of this is that both have access to the Father by one and the same Spirit. There isn't a Spirit for Jews and a Spirit for gentiles; both approach God through the same Spirit, thus obliterating segregation.

Being filled with the Spirit is not simply a matter of exhibiting gifts and living a holy life, as if those things were simple, but in addition to these aspects there is a focus on unity. Paul writes to the Ephesians that he wishes them to be "eager to maintain the unity of the Spirit in the bond of peace"[489]. Paul then equates the singular hope they have in Christ with the singularity of the Spirit and the body[490]; he insists that there can be no permission for divisions in the church, as there is one body and one Spirit, not several of each. Paul links the singularity of the hope of the gospel with the singularity of the church and Spirit.

On the other side of this teaching, Jude describes people who are worldly and cause divisions as being "devoid of the Spirit"[491]. This somewhat damning verdict of people who cause divisions in churches shows the seriousness with which divisions are regarded. As if to doubly make the point, Jude goes on to urge the church to keep themselves in the love of God by "building [themselves] up in your most holy faith and praying in the Holy Spirit"[492]. Building oneself up in the most holy faith means to remind oneself, and one

---

[488] Ephesians 2:18
[489] Ephesians 4:3
[490] Ephesians 4:4
[491] Jude 1:19
[492] Jude 1:20-21

another, of the hope we have in Christ, and also to be praying in the Holy Spirit. This is important, as the church is comprised of those who have "tasted the most holy gift and who have shared in the Holy Spirit"[493], and the purpose of these things is to be built together into a dwelling place for God by the Holy Spirit[494]. This kind of dwelling place is to be free of divisions.

## Conclusions

When thinking about the Spirit in these roles, we are struck by a number of points. Firstly, when reading through the references to the Spirit convicting and converting people, we must conclude that there is no set 'layout' or 'order' to the manner by which these occur. Sometimes baptism in water happens first, sometimes the coming of the Spirit happens first, and sometimes they are synonymous. This must steer us away from having any set order that we insist conversion happen by; if Scripture doesn't insist upon a particular order, neither should we.

This brings us to a second application; we must be ever-vigilant to keep a healthy, Biblical balance between insisting that the gospel comes about by words and that the gospel comes about by power. All too many churches will insist upon one at the expense of the other. This is not to say that one without the other will have no worth or that taking this perspective will kill the effect of the gospel; both carry the power of God unto salvation. However, omitting the power of the gospel by signs and wonders will leave us with an intellectual faith, with little or no expectation of God to manifest or act. Equally, omitting the power of the gospel by the preached and taught word will leave the church with an experiential faith, comfortable with the miraculous but ignorant of the doctrines which underpin it. Such a faith will leave believers with little to cling to when tribulations come and unable to defend their perspective, as Peter and James write that we should be able to[495]. To release the

---

[493] Hebrews 6:4
[494] Ephesians 2:22

163

true power of the gospel, we must embody both the written word and the miraculous power of the gospel together in one church.

Finally, we must never use the Spirit, and what we believe about His work and ministry, to tear down other believers, churches or denominations. I fear and suspect that much tearing down takes place online these days, and if a person dislikes or disagrees with a certain type of church, there are usually a dozen more to which this person can go. We must be especially careful that when we disagree with other people's beliefs, we do not lose our brothers in order to win an argument. Such is the manner Jesus requires of us when dealing with people's errors[496]. One of the Spirit's remits is to build up the church, not to tear her down. If certain people are in serious error and are unwilling to listen to sound reason from a good heart, it is not up to us to convince them; Christ will do that. Rather, keeping in step with the Spirit, we should continue to love and build up people with whom we disagree. We cannot just love those with whom we agree; even the tax collectors do that![497]

---

[495] 1 Peter 3:15, James 3:17
[496] Matthew 18:15
[497] Matthew 5:46

# Eleven

# The Spirit Inspires

## ✳✳✳

If you were to ask a cessationist Christian what they believe the Spirit did (back when He was active, from the perspective that He is no longer so), they would probably reply that the Spirit was the inspiration of the Bible, quoting 2 Timothy 3:16. Even for those of us who do not subscribe to the cessationist position, this naturally raises a question; is His inspiration of Scripture the extent of the Spirit's inspirational activity, or are there other examples of His inspirational work? We can turn to the Old Testament to see that the Spirit isn't only a writer of holy books, but also an inspiration to those who would speak the words of God.

### The Spirit Inspires in the Old Testament

In the book of Numbers, we read of the Spirit inspiring the oracles of Balaam. Balaam was known as someone who could influence the outcome of a battle or military campaign by using his gift as an oracle; those whom Balaam chose to curse would be cursed, and those whom he was to bless would be blessed[498]. During Balaam's third oracle in Numbers 24, it is said that the Spirit of God came upon him[499], and Balaam prophesied as "the oracle of him who hears the words of God, who sees the vision of the Almighty."[500] This caused great frustration for Balak, the man who had hired Balaam in order to defeat Israel by using his oracles!

---

[498] Numbers 22:6
[499] Numbers 24:2
[500] Numbers 24:4

This tells us something about the nature of the inspiration of the Spirit; when a person is inspired to speak by the Spirit, their words are not their own. They will often speak in their own language, but what they utter is given by Almighty God as definitive truth. In the case of Balaam, he received a change of mind in the midst of his oracle, whereby he declared that it is the LORD, and not himself, about whom people can say, "Blessed are those who bless you, and cursed are those who curse you"[501]. While we should be careful in equating Old Testament with New Testament prophecy, I believe there is a line of similarity between them; they both contain the words of God, and are therefore entirely true 100% of the time. As we have seen in chapter 3, in the new covenant era we are instructed to weigh prophecy before accepting it as the direct instructions of the Lord. When someone's words are clearly their own, I believe we should weigh their words all the more carefully. However, if we have weighed prophecy and are convinced that their words are God's words, we should submit to their wisdom.

In 2 Samuel 23 we read of the "last words of David"[502]. These are, in fact, not the last words of David, as he does speak in chapter 24. Rather, these supposed last words of David are in fact the final *oracle* of David; his last words uttered under the inspiration of the Spirit. Interestingly, and helpfully for our purposes, his opening words of this oracle reaffirm the origin of these words;

> "The Spirit of the LORD speaks by me; his word is on my tongue"[503].

This adds weight to the assertion that when the Spirit inspires someone to speak, that person speaks the LORD's very words.

When viewed in this light, the action of speaking the very words of God makes more sense of the third of the 'Ten Commandments'.

---

501 Numbers 24:9
502 2 Samuel 23:1
503 2 Samuel 23:2

Exodus 20:7 instructs God's people not to take the name of the LORD in vain, which is, I believe, often interpreted wrongly. For a long time I believed that this meant to avoid the phrase 'oh my God', and variations thereof, as an expression of anger or frustration. However, thinking through this interpretation with a fresh perspective, it makes very little sense. Why would God be so concerned with preventing His people from using one individual phrase that He made it the third commandment for them to follow? It seems an awfully specific rule to impose upon people, and it truly seems out of place in alongside 'have no other gods before me' and 'you shall not commit murder'.

There is a clue in the meaning of the word translated as 'vain'. The Hebrew word 'shav' connotes 'emptiness' and 'falsehood'. In the case of Exodus 20, this would refer to emptiness of speech, or, in other words, lying. So, when the commandment states that we should not take the LORD's name in vain, I believe the strongest interpretation would be along the lines of 'Do not claim that the LORD said something to you when He did no such thing'. This turns the commandment away from avoiding an innocuous phrase to a matter of character; God is quite adamant that any words attributed to Him are actually His.

When David was king, there arose a curious and pleasant phrase used to describe someone being inspired by the Holy Spirit. Amasai, one of David's 'mighty men', is said to have been "clothed in the Spirit of God"[504]. The same phrase is used in 2 Chronicles to describe the inspiration of Zechariah, son of Jehoiada the priest[505]. Describing someone as 'clothed in the Spirit of God' implies a closeness between the person and the Spirit; if I am wearing a coat, I am very close to that garment. Its movements are my movements. Similarly, there if someone is clothed with the Spirit, there is a connection between the

---

[504] 1 Chronicles 12:18
[505] 2 Chronicles 24:20

person and the Spirit. In these verses, the words uttered by these people are the words of the Spirit.

During the time of the Kings, while Jehoshaphat is king of Judah and Ahab is king of Israel, a fist-fight breaks out concerning the inspiration of the LORD. King Ahab summons Micaiah, who is renowned for being able to inquire of the LORD, and Micaiah does just this[506]. This summoning somewhat treads on the toes of one of the other prophets, Zedekiah, who punches Micaiah in the face, asking "How did the Spirit of the LORD go from me to speak to you?"[507] The parallel account in 2 Chronicles renders this as "Which way did the Spirit of the LORD go from me to speak to you?[508]" While Zedekiah wrongly believed that the Spirit of God was his own possession, his understanding of the Spirit's inspiration was fundamentally right. Zedekiah realised that a person cannot simply speak in their own strength, rather they must do so by the inspiration of the Spirit, if their utterance is to be classed as the word of the LORD.

There is ample evidence from the Old Testament to point to the Spirit's inspiration of the prophets. We read in 2 Chronicles;

> "And the Spirit of the LORD came upon Jahaziel the son of Zechariah ... in the midst of the assembly. And he said, "Listen, all Judah and inhabitants of Jerusalem and King Jehoshaphat: Thus says the LORD to you, 'Do not be afraid and do not be dismayed at this great horde, for the battle is not yours but God's"[509].

While Jahaziel isn't strictly one of the prophets who wrote any Biblical books, he does use the phrase uttered by the prophets when bringing the words of God, "Thus says the LORD to you". This,

---

[506] 1 Kings 22:8
[507] 1 Kings 22:24
[508] 2 Chronicles 18:23
[509] 2 Chronicles 20:14

combined with the mention of the Spirit of the LORD coming upon Jahaziel, points us to the conclusion that he was speaking the words of God.

In the book of Nehemiah, after Ezra has read the book of law and the people of Israel have confessed their sins, the Levites give a rousing overview of the journey the people have been on with God[510]. Towards the end of this, they tell us that God bore with the people for many years and "warned them by your Spirit through your prophets. Yet they would not give ear"[511]. With a similar sentiment, the prophet Zechariah tells us that the people;

> "...made their hearts diamond-hard lest they should hear the law and the words that the LORD of hosts had sent by his Spirit through the former prophets"[512].

These verses from 2 Chronicles, Nehemiah, and Zechariah confirm the assertion that the Old Testament prophets were speaking by the inspiration of the Holy Spirit. This means that, since the prophets brought the words of God, then this is how God chooses to communicate with people; through the inspiring Holy Spirit.

**The Spirit Inspires in the New Testament**

Even when we come to the New Testament we find references to the Spirit-inspired nature of the Old. When Jesus was quizzing the Pharisees about whom they thought the Christ would be, they answer that he will be the son of David. Jesus then replied, asking "How is it then that David, in the Spirit, calls him Lord?"[513] quoting Psalm 110. Jesus has no trouble in describing the words that David wrote as being 'in the Spirit', pointing to their divine inspiration by the third person of the Trinity.

---

[510] Nehemiah 9:5
[511] Nehemiah 9:30
[512] Zechariah 7:12
[513] Matthew 22:43, Mark 12:36

The apostles present a similar view of the divine authority of Scripture in Acts, when they are discussing the betrayal of Judas and the necessity to replace him among the twelve. When making reference to Psalms 69 and 109, they say that;

> "...the Scripture had to be fulfilled, which the Holy Spirit spoke beforehand by the mouth of David concerning Judas."[514]

This verse contains three important points; firstly that the Scriptures were written by the Holy Spirit, secondly that the Scriptures were written by the Holy Spirit 'by the mouth of David', their human author, and finally that the Spirit is outside of time as He was able to inspire David to write about Judas 1,000 years before the event.

After Peter and John had spoken before the council in Acts 4, they return to their friends and quote from Psalm 2, the words of God spoken "through the mouth of our father David, your servant, said by the Holy Spirit"[515]. The writer to the Hebrews quotes Psalm 95, introducing it with the phrase "Therefore, as the Holy Spirit says..."[516] Finally, at the end of the book of Acts, when Paul is in under house arrest in Rome, he quotes the book of Isaiah, saying;

> "The Holy Spirit was right in saying to your fathers through Isaiah the prophet..."[517]

These New Testament references to the Spirit inspiring David to write the Psalms tell us two things; firstly, the apostles had no trouble in believing that the Old Testament was the very word of God, and secondly, that they sought to understand everything that was happening to them in light of the Scriptures they had at the time.

---

[514] Acts 1:16
[515] Acts 4:25
[516] Hebrews 3:7
[517] Acts 28:25

The majority of references to the Spirit inspiring people in the New Testament are concerned with the Spirit giving someone words to say, either as a direct instruction from God, or else giving them wisdom to know what to say in a difficult circumstance. Jesus mentions this second example in Mark 13, describing that when his followers are hauled in front of councils and governors on account of their faith in Him, they shouldn't worry about what they are to say in this moment, because the Holy Spirit will give you things to speak in that hour[518]. Although this passage is in the context of the signs of the end of the age, Jesus words have the ring of immediate truth; we see them fulfilled in Acts 4 with Peter and John, as well as with Stephen in Acts 7. As such, we should not relegate His words to matters exclusively concerning the end times, but we should embrace them as a comfort when we face difficult circumstances because of our faith.

Stephen's arrest and speech in Acts 6-7 is but one of a number of examples in the New Testament where people spoke according to what the Spirit was instructing them to say. Luke writes of those listening to Stephen as he speaks, who ultimately incite the elders and scribes to have him arrested, that they "could not withstand the wisdom and the Spirit with which he was speaking"[519]. Jesus affirms that those who are sent by God are given words from God, because, as He puts it, "...He gives the Spirit without measure"[520]. Additionally, the very commands given by Jesus to the Apostles after His resurrection are described as being "given through the Holy Spirit."[521]

There are two final references that we haven't explored which are arguably the most memorable on the issue of the Spirit inspiring. We find one in Ephesians 6, where Paul writes about the full armour of God. He describes the method by which Christians can do battle against the "cosmic powers over this present darkness, against the

---

[518] Mark 13:11
[519] Acts 6:10
[520] John 3:34
[521] Acts 1:2

spiritual forces of evil..."[522] After mentioning truth, righteousness, peace, faith and salvation, Paul instructs us to,

> "...take up ... the sword of the Spirit, which is the word of God, praying at all times in the Spirit, with all prayer and supplication"[523].

Given what we've seen of the Spirit inspiring the Scriptures, which is made explicitly clear concerning the Old Testament and very implicitly clear about the New[524], Paul personalises them from something that is objectively true into something which is personally useful. This passage in Ephesians reminds us that the Christian life is not one of skipping through fields with Jesus singing worship songs, but rather that we are in a war. We are not in a war of flesh and blood, whereby our enemies are those marked by their wearing a different coloured uniform, rather, we have an unseen enemy, one who cannot be shot with an arrow or negotiated with. The book of Revelation tells us the outcome of this war – Jesus wins – but also that it will be long and bloody and costly.

Here in Ephesians 6, Paul is invoking his readers not to be ignorant of this spiritual truth, but to defend and arm themselves with spiritual equipment. The main offensive weapon is the sword of the Spirit; the word of God. Rightly used – praying at all times in the Spirit when using it – the Scriptures are the very words of God and the enemy cannot withstand them. This does not mean that those wielding the sword will have an automatic victory – Jesus himself quoted Deuteronomy three times over 40 days before the devil left him[525] – but it does mean that the Christian doesn't go into the battle unprepared and unarmed. The word of God is the sword of

---

[522] Ephesians 6:12
[523] Ephesians 6:16 - 18
[524] For a more detailed explanation of the Divine Inspiration of the New Testament documents, see W. Grudem, *Systematic Theology*, pp 73 - 77
[525] Matthew 4:1-11

the Spirit. Paul is here establishing the link between the written word of the Bible and the divine inspiration of the Spirit who authored it.

This leads us to our final reference; 2 Timothy 3:16 is the cornerstone verse of protestant Christianity.

> "All Scripture is breathed out by God and profitable for teaching, for reproof, for correction, and for training in righteousness, that the man of God may be complete, equipped for every good work"[526].

While not explicitly mentioning the Holy Spirit, the choice of Greek words here is revealing of what Paul believed about the inspiration of Scripture. The words which we read as 'breathed out by God' are actually all from one single Greek word *'theopneustos'*. This word is unique in Scripture, and is derived from the roots of the Greek words for 'God' and for 'wind'. The Greek word for 'Spirit', *'pneuma'*, is the same word for 'wind', and is used interchangeably. Take John 3:8 for example;

> "The wind blows where it wishes, and you hear its sound, but you do not know where it comes from or where it goes. So it is with everyone who is born of the Spirit"[527].

The Greek word used for 'wind' at the beginning of the verse is the very same Greek word used for 'Spirit' at the end of the verse. It would have been incumbent upon the original Greek reader to determine which interpretation Jesus, the speaker, and John, the author, were meaning with each usage. Moving back to 2 Timothy, the unique nature of this word makes it difficult, though not impossible, to understand the intended meaning. However, given that the roots of this word are 'God' and 'wind', it is not too far of a stretch to conclude that it is God the Holy Spirit who is inspiring Scripture. The purpose of this inspiration of *all* Scripture is included

---

[526] 2 Timothy 3:16-17
[527] John 3:8

within the verse; that we may be equipped for every good work. The divine authorship of the Bible is not an end in itself, but rather is a means to doing something else; good works. The avenue by which God's people are brought to doing these good works is by being taught, corrected, reproofed and trained in righteousness by this Holy book. We should pay attention to Scripture because the Holy Spirit inspired it to be written. We should pay attention to the inspiration of the Spirit because the Bible says so much about it.

**Conclusion**

Given that we have firmly established the fact that the Spirit inspires people to do, say or write things, what are we to do about this? Firstly, I believe that every church and every Christian needs to acknowledge that the inspiration of the Holy Spirit is not to be demoted to an historical fact, but rather must be realised as a contemporary truth. Since we see examples of the Spirit inspiring people in the Old Testament, in the life of Jesus, in the ministry of the apostles and in their instructions to the churches they looked after, we would be remiss in overlooking the inspiration of the Spirit in our own contemporary churches. While the canon of Scripture is closed[528] and the Spirit will not be inspiring any further Biblical books, the Spirit's inspiration for God's people to say or do certain things continues to this day.

Secondly, while keeping this first point in mind, it is important to also acknowledge that not everyone who claims to speak the words of God actually does so. It is not so very difficult to think of times when we have heard or heard of someone speaking "the words of the Lord" but is actually speaking something short of that. Being confident of what one is saying does not make one theologically

---

[528] At least, because the Bible ends with the book of Revelation, we can say that there will be no further Biblical books until after the new heavens and the new earth are established at the return of Christ. I believe it is unlikely that any further biblical books will be needed once God dwells with His people.

correct. To this end, it is vitally important to weigh everything that is said which claims to be the words of God. The Spirit does inspire people today, but we must be wise as well as faithful. If what is being said clearly contradicts Scripture, it must be disregarded. If what is being said seems to be in line with Scripture, but the Spirit living inside you does not resonate with it, then it should be prayed over. The Spirit does not contradict Himself. However, if what is being said is in line with Scripture and the Spirit within you gives a resounding "yes and amen!", then rejoice and follow the inspiring word of the Spirit of God!

Finally, what we have seen from our Biblical survey of the Spirit's inspiring ministry is that this is very rarely an end in itself. When the Spirit inspires someone, it is almost always to say or do something. This means that we must do more than internalise an interesting theological truth; rather, we must act when the Spirit prompts us to act. This could be speaking to that person who you've been avoiding, it could be starting to do something for someone or a cause which you've not done yet or it could even be to move one's whole life to another place for the sake of the kingdom of God. This is why we need to listen for and act upon the inspiring Holy Spirit; while he calls each of us, He calls each of us differently.

# Twelve

# The Spirit is with you

## ✳✳✳

In this final chapter, we will examine the biblical basis for a phrase commonly used by evangelical, charismatic and Pentecostal Christians. Among these groups of Christians is where we are most likely to hear the phrase, "so-and-so has a particular anointing." The particularities of the anointing in question will vary from person to person, but we can often hear talk of an anointing of healing, an anointing of service, an anointing of preaching or an anointing of evangelism. As with so much of Christian jargon, applying a word we find in the Bible regularly[529] to contemporary expressions of church *can* lead to the biblical meaning getting lost in translation, resulting in a catch-all phrase which is used interchangeably with other words, but being completely devoid of the word's original meaning. I believe that what is meant by use of this particular phrase is that the Spirit is believed to be with someone in a personal and powerful way, which results in their excelling in their gifting. In our quest to understand the Holy Spirit, we must examine how and why He anoints particular people. This final chapter will investigate the instances where the Spirit rests upon certain people, anointing them with Himself.

### The Spirit was with people in the Old Testament

The first instance of the Spirit resting on someone in the Old Testament is found in Numbers. We have already made reference to this story in chapter 3, but we find within it the phrase we are currently seeking to understand;

---

[529] Various Greek and Hebrew words rendered as 'anoint' or 'anointing' appear in the Bible more than 150 times.

"Now two men remained in the camp, one named Eldad, and the other named Medad, and the Spirit rested on them."[530]

This verse gives us pause to consider the words we are reading here. The Hebrew word for 'rested' in this verse is 'nuwach', and is translated as 'to settle down and remain'. This does not necessarily imply the lack of activity, but rather the closeness of knowing someone is with you who calms and quiets your soul. This is the type of fellowship Eldad and Medad enjoyed with the Spirit. If we read on in this passage for a few more verses, we see that they do go on to prophesy[531], but the order in which they do so is telling; they rested with the Spirit before they acted in the Spirit.

During the time of the judges, the people of Israel did what was evil in the sight of the LORD by intermarrying with Canaanites, the Hittites, the Amorites, the Perizzites, the Hivites, and the Jebusites, and served their respective gods[532]. As is so often the pattern of the relationship between the people of Israel and their LORD, they soon forgot about Him until they found themselves in the midst of disaster, in this instance being ruled by a foreign king. They cry out to the LORD, who raises up a deliverer named Othniel for the people. We read that the Spirit was upon him, and he judged Israel, went out to war against their captors and prevailed over them. As a result of this, the land had rest for forty years[533].

The way this story is laid out in the book of Judges makes it look like it was a quick episode as it occupies only a handful of verses. However, these events would have taken place over about a decade. We're not told how long it was between Othniel being raised up and him defeating the oppressive Cushan-rishathaim. We're also not told how long the Spirit rested upon him before he went out to war. But

---

[530] Numbers 11:26
[531] Numbers 11:26 – 29
[532] Judges 3:5-6
[533] Judges 3:7-11

the order in which the events happen is quite clear; first the Spirit rested on him, then he judged Israel, then he mounted a victorious military campaign. Again we see an explicit order here; Othniel rested in and with the Spirit before taking up arms.

We have already examined the phrase 'the Spirit of the LORD rushed upon so-and-so' in chapter 3. We will now revisit 1 Samuel 16, where the Spirit rushes upon David as he is anointed king. Remember, this happened many years before he was *appointed* as king, which gives weight to the belief that God's view of time is often quite different from ours.

> "Then Samuel took the horn of oil and anointed him in the midst of his brothers. And the Spirit of the LORD rushed upon David from that day forward... Now the Spirit of the LORD departed from Saul..."[534]

These verses deconstruct the increasingly popular belief that the Spirit of God is present in every human being, regardless of whether or not they are saved. When Samuel anoints David as the future king of Israel, the Spirit of the LORD rushes upon David 'from that day forward'. This implies that *this* was the beginning of a series of events which continued long after the oil had drained away. Equally, the very next verse tells us that the Spirit departed from Saul from that time. This one event of David being anointed brings about the beginning of David's walk with the Spirit and the end of Saul's.

Transferring this truth into a new covenant context is not straightforward, as now the Spirit has been poured out and made available to all at Pentecost. However, the person of the Spirit has not changed from the days of Samuel to today, and so we must translate the story appropriately. Not every person today has the Holy Spirit as a companion, but every Christian does. Through the work of Christ on the cross, every Christian is favoured by God

---

[534] 1 Samuel 16:13-14

because Christ is favoured by God. In 1 Samuel 16, David is favoured of God and so has the Spirit, whereas because of his actions in 1 Samuel 15, Saul is no longer favoured by God, and so the Spirit departs from him. Failing to make this distinction, between those who are favoured of God and those who are not, in our new covenant context leads us to a belief that all people are, or will be, saved, which the Bible simply does not support[535].

Ezekiel gives us some pause to consider this activity of the Spirit. We read in Ezekiel 3 that the Spirit of the LORD enters him, which we have already mentioned in chapter 8 in the context of the Spirit filling or indwelling, but for our current purposes we must consider this verse again. We are told that the Spirit enters into Ezekiel and sets him on his feet before "speaking with him"[536]. What is interesting in this verse is the variety of facets which the Spirit seems to express here; first entering *into* Ezekiel, then physically *moving* him, then speaking *with* him. Notice that the writer, presumably Ezekiel himself, refers to this event as the Spirit speaking *with* him and not *to* him. This points us more to the idea that the Spirit is a person to converse with, rather than a force one is compelled to listen to. This verse is prefaced two verses earlier by the Ezekiel saying that "the hand of the LORD was upon me there"[537]. The following verse tells us that Ezekiel then encounters the glory of the LORD, before the Spirit enters him and speaks with him. It does seem that verse 24, where the Spirit meets and speaks with him, is the fulfilment of verse 22, where the hand of the LORD was upon him and compelled him to go to where the glory of the LORD would overwhelm him.

The book of Isaiah gives us two different glimpses of the Spirit being with people, specifically a prophesy of how the Spirit would be on

---

[535] See Daniel 12:2, Matthew 25:31-46, John 5:29, Revelation 20:12-13, etc.
[536] Ezekiel 3:24
[537] Ezekiel 3:22

and with Jesus. The first of these is in chapter 42, where the LORD says;

> "Behold my servant, whom I uphold, my chosen, in whom my soul delights; I have put my Spirit upon him; he will bring forth justice to the nations"[538].

This is actually a rather beautiful insight into the relationship the Father has with the Son; "the one in whom my soul delights". The usage of both the present tense, "I have put my Spirit upon him" and the future tense, "he will bring forth justice to the nations" implies someone who is, was and is to come. This person has the Spirit of the LORD upon Him. Isaiah elaborates on this later on in chapter 61, where we see a messianic picture of what the year of the LORD's favour will look like.

> "The Spirit of the Lord GOD is upon me, because the LORD has anointed me to bring good news to the poor; he has sent me to bind up the broken-hearted, to proclaim liberty to the captives, and the opening of the prison to those who are bound"[539].

This is, of course, the Scripture which Jesus quotes in Luke 4 while in the synagogue at Nazareth[540]. The original passage from Isaiah speaks of the person in question bringing good news to the poor, binding up the broken hearted and proclaiming liberty to captives. These are the results of this person's ministry, which are brought about by the LORD anointing him with the Spirit of the LORD. The implications of this are rather clear from both this passage and it's fulfilment in Luke 4; action for the kingdom of God must come after waiting on the anointing of the Spirit of God.

---

[538] Isaiah 42:1
[539] Isaiah 61:1
[540] Luke 4:16-19

## The Spirit is with people in the New Testament era

When Jesus was a baby, the custom of Moses meant that He, being the first born, must be presented at the temple, in accordance with Exodus 13:2, and Mary and Joseph made a sacrifice there. In Jerusalem lived a man named Simeon, who had been promised that he would not die before he had seen the messiah. Simeon was righteous, devout and the Holy Spirit was upon him[541]. He came "in the Spirit into the temple"[542], took the baby Jesus in his arms and blessed God for seeing Him. This man had waited patiently, with the Holy Spirit, for something which could only be accomplished through God's direct action. Simeon is described as righteous and devout. If indeed the Spirit was with Simeon from the time he was promised to behold the messiah, then we could conclude that His constant companionship with Simeon resulted in him being described as righteous and devout. We become like whom we fellowship with. This is not an automatic happening; fellowship with someone has to be intentional, but if it is we will begin to resemble those we are around.

When Jesus is a grown man, he approaches John to be baptised by him in the Jordan. John initially refuses, but Jesus wins him over. We read in both the Gospel of Luke and of John that "the Holy Spirit descended on him in bodily form, like a dove"[543] and that "it remained on him"[544]. John the Baptist tells us that the one who sent him to baptise with water explained that the person upon whom the Spirit descended *and remained* would be the one who would baptise with Holy Spirit[545]. The word for 'baptise' is a transliteration from the word *'baptizo'*, meaning to immerse, submerge or overwhelm the item or person in question. It is used to describe the sinking of a ship; the ship was overwhelmed with the water, just as the person

---

[541] Luke 2:25
[542] Luke 2:27
[543] Luke 3:22
[544] John 1:32
[545] John 1:33

being baptised with the Holy Spirit is overwhelmed with the Spirit. John's words are a foreshadowing of Pentecost, when the believers are filled with the Holy Spirit, but they also bring to mind Jesus' words in John 7, where he explains that...

> "Whoever believes in me, as the Scripture has said, 'Out of his heart will flow rivers of living water.'" Now this he said about the Spirit, whom those who believed in him were to receive, for as yet the Spirit had not been given, because Jesus was not yet glorified"[546].

This verse gives a timeframe for the events John the Baptist was talking about in John 1; Jesus would baptise with Holy Spirit, this would be an immersion of the believer in Him, but this hadn't happened at that point because Jesus had not yet been glorified.

This event tells us several things about the Holy Spirit. We have already discussed the symbolism of the Spirit coming as a dove in chapter 4, but the fact that it is specifically noted that the dove remained on Him is interesting. This was the first time that this had happened. While those watching this event could not have known it at the time, the Spirit remaining on Jesus was evident to the Gospel writers several decades later. Jesus was the first person to have the Spirit descend on Him and stay with Him always. We see this in Luke 4, where Jesus returns from the wilderness "in the Power of the Spirit", i.e., with the Spirit still with Him. There is much evidence for the Spirit remaining with Jesus throughout his entire ministry.

In Matthew 12, Jesus says that the kingdom has come upon those listening to him because he casts out demons by the Spirit of God, showing that he did this by the Holy Spirit[547]. The book of Acts has Peter describing Jesus as being anointed with the Holy Spirit and with power to "do good" and heal all who were oppressed of the devil[548], and the book of Romans says that Jesus was declared to be

---

[546] John 7:38 - 39
[547] Matthew 12:28

the Son of God in power "according to the Spirit of holiness"[549]. Paul writes of Christ that he was "He was manifested in the flesh, vindicated by the Spirit..."[550]. This means that he was declared to be righteous by the Spirit, presumably by the Spirit resting on Him. I do not believe that this verse causes us to conclude that Christ was *made to be righteous* by the Spirit, implying that there was a time when He was not righteous[551], but rather that through the Spirit resting on Jesus he was *declared* to be righteous to those around Him. Such is the ministry of the Spirit.

These verses lead us to the conclusion that Jesus, during His earthly ministry, enjoyed the fellowship of the Holy Spirit from the moment of His baptism by John until the crucifixion; He lived a life with the Spirit as his companion. This companionship spurred him to action, as we read about in Luke 4.

We mentioned earlier the passage from Isaiah 61 which declares that the LORD's anointed would proclaim good news to the poor, bind up the broken hearted, liberty to captives, recovery of sight to the blind and the year of the LORD's favour. After Jesus' baptism and temptation he returns home to Nazareth and reads this scroll in the synagogue, before declaring, "Today this Scripture has been fulfilled in your hearing"[552]. This caused something of an uproar in the synagogue, because the people gathered here had known Jesus growing up as Joseph the carpenters' son, and here He was proclaiming that he was the LORD's anointed one with the Spirit upon Him. They drove him out of town and tried to throw Him of a cliff for such blasphemy. However, what Jesus went on to do proved the validity of these claims; He did proclaim good news to the poor, liberty to captives and recovery of sight to the blind! His actions

---

[548] Acts 10:38
[549] Romans 1:4
[550] 1 Timothy 3:16
[551] Verses such as 2 Corinthians 5:21 and Hebrews 4:15 give us evidence to the contrary.
[552] Luke 4:21

proved that He was the LORD's anointed and that the Spirit of the LORD was upon Him.

The book of Acts gives us a glimpse into the role of those who lead the Christian church. When Paul is speaking to the leaders of the Ephesian church, he explains that "the Holy Spirit has made you overseers, to care for the church of God, which he obtained with his own blood"[553]. Here we have a Trinitarian statement about the church. The church belongs to God the Father, which the Son purchased with His blood and whom the Holy Spirit has made certain people to be overseers of. This tells us that those who oversee the church aren't called on sole account of their intellect, personality or even skills, but that it is the Holy Spirit who makes them overseers. We should learn to recognise this calling when appointing church leaders.

However, you don't need to be a Christian for very long to have experienced the difficulties Jesus promised will befall those who follow him[554].

> "If you are insulted for the name of Christ, you are blessed, because the Spirit of glory and of God rests upon you"[555].

There are at least two ways of reading this verse. The first would say that the Spirit of glory and of God rests upon a person *because* he or she is insulted for the name of Christ. Many sincere Christians would hold this view, and there is indeed some weight to it. Jesus did say that in this world there would be troubles[556], and "woe to you when all people speak well of you"[557]. Many Christians over the years have embraced troubles as a sign that they are indeed following Christ, who suffered more than anyone on the cross. However, this verse

---

[553] Acts 20:28
[554] John 16:33, Revelation 1:9, Acts 14:22
[555] 1 Peter 4:14
[556] John 16:33
[557] Luke 6:26

can be read simply as a reminder that when these troubles come, to remember that you are blessed, and that the Spirit of glory and God rests on you. The chapter of 1 Peter in question has verses like "do not be surprised at the fiery trial when it comes upon you to test you"[558], and "But rejoice insofar as you share Christ's sufferings..."[559] These tell us that though suffering is not something to be sought out, if we encounter it we can rejoice. I believe the linchpin to this conundrum is the Spirit of glory resting upon us. In our own strength, we would have to be foolish or mad to rejoice in suffering, but through the strength of the Spirit living within us and resting on us, we can face anything the world can throw at us, and even rejoice.

**Conclusion**

So what are we to do in light of this biblical certainty that the Spirit is with us? Firstly, I believe the Christian church needs to get better at following Jesus' commandment in Luke 24, which echoes the example of many faithful people in the Old Testament. The disciples have witnessed the crucifixion, witnessed the resurrection and had Jesus appear to them in a locked room. His last words to His disciples in the gospel of Luke are;

"I am sending the promise of my Father upon you. But stay in the city until you are clothed with power from on high"[560].

One of the most important aspects of correctly understanding a verse is to look at the verses which came before it and after it. Jesus had defeated sin and death and has risen victoriously from the dead; still He tells His disciples, the first eye-witnesses of this, to wait until they have been clothed with power from on high. I believe that we in the 21st century need to learn to be patient. All too regularly we rush into activity without waiting to be clothed with power from on high.

---

[558] 1 Peter 4:12
[559] 1 Peter 4:13
[560] Luke 24:49

Action should be the product of knowing, believing and experiencing the Spirit with us.

Secondly, while it is true that the Spirit dwells within us and indeed is also with us, this does not mean that every Christian is automatically totally sanctified. Sanctification, the process of becoming more like Jesus, is a process which happens over the whole of our lives. However, in a spiritual as well as in a social sense, we become like whom we associate with. If we spend a lot of time with someone who is violent, our thoughts, if not our behaviour, will begin to be accepting and even approving of violence. On the other hand, if we associate with someone who is generous, the same principle applies, and we will find our thoughts, feelings and actions may become more generous. Concerning the Spirit, if we spend time with the Spirit of God, we will become more like Him. The fruit of the Spirit is a phrase used to mean the product of the Spirit; love, joy, peace, patience, goodness, kindness, gentleness, faithfulness and self-control[561]. In this manner, when we face persecution, in whatever form that might be, relying more on the Spirit's comfort and guidance rather than what 'common sense' would have us believe will make the persecution bearable, and even profitable. Fellowshipping with the Spirit must be intentional on our part, for He is always with us. We must simply make time for Him.

---

[561] Galatians 5:22-23

# Thirteen

# Conclusion and Application

### ✳✳✳

Up until this point, we could have been surveying the entire Bible and exegeting some 300 verses concerning the Holy Spirit, and yet come away with our minds stimulated but without it having any effect on our lives. If this were to be the case, I would have entirely failed in my purpose of bringing understanding which leads to transformation. What I have been seeking to do is to untie some unbiblical beliefs concerning the Holy Spirit, and to replace them with more accurate, Biblical ones. Each of the preceding chapters has a small conclusion of its own included within it, and I do not wish to simply copy and paste these. Rather, I want to summarise and apply to our lives what we have learnt in our epic biblical journey. The following is a short-hand version of what we have already discussed in the previous dozen chapters.

<u>Twenty Things to Consider</u>

**One: The gifts of the Spirit are to be used to bring Glory to God.** Using them for any other purpose cuts across the very reason why they are given. We must wield the power of the Spirit wisely. **Application:** Avoid going astray by continually seeking God and evaluating your motives for using His gifts. If our motives stray from honourable and holy ones, we need to repent of this and seek the giver of the gifts afresh.

**Two: The gifts of the Spirit are for every believer.** One of the fallacies that can crop up in charismatic church is that the gifts listed in Ephesians 4 (apostle, prophet, evangelist, pastor and teacher) are the sum total of the gifts of the Spirit. Actually, there is a much broader range of gifts of the Spirit than these 5, which we should be attentive to. An exhaustive list contains;

> Intercession[562], prophecy[563], serving[564], teaching[565], exhortation, giving, leadership, mercy[566], celibacy, marriage[567], word of knowledge, word of wisdom[568], faith[569], healing[570], miracles[571], discernment of spirits[572], speaking in tongues[573], interpretation of tongues[574], apostle[575], administration[576], evangelist, pastor[577] and hospitality[578].

**Application:** Given the variety of these gifts, and keeping in mind Paul's line of questioning in 1 Corinthians 12 which asserts that not everyone has every gift, churches should be seeking to bring every gift into fruition in equal measure. Anything short of this suggests, either explicitly or implicitly, that certain gifts are more special or worthy than others. Paul's analogy of the body in the same chapter lends weight to this; there are some parts of the body which are more obvious or get more attention, but to lose any one part will affect the whole being. Similarly, a church which emphasises

---

[562] Romans 8:26-27
[563] Romans 12:6, 1 Corinthians 12:10, 1 Corinthians 12:28, Ephesians 4:11
[564] Romans 12:7, 1 Corinthians 12:28
[565] Romans 12:7, 1 Corinthians 12:28, Ephesians 4:11
[566] Romans 12:8
[567] 1 Corinthians 7:7
[568] 1 Corinthians 12:8
[569] 1 Corinthians 12:9
[570] 1 Corinthians 12:9, 1 Corinthians 12:28
[571] 1 Corinthians 12:10, 1 Corinthians 12:28
[572] 1 Corinthians 12:10
[573] 1 Corinthians 12:10, 1 Corinthians 12:28
[574] 1 Corinthians 12:10
[575] 1 Corinthians 12:28, Ephesians 4:11
[576] 1 Corinthians 12:28
[577] Ephesians 4:11
[578] 1 Peter 4:9

prophecy or teaching or evangelism or healing over all the other gifts may see much fruit in that area, but those members of the church which don't have that gift may become frustrated and bitter, and their gift may wither. As a result, the fruit that gift would garner may be absent.

**Three: The Spirit is diverse.** Because of this considerable variety of gifts of the Spirit, and indeed because the Spirit is a person and not a formula, how the Spirit will act in one situation may well differ from how He acts in the next one. **Application:** When we find ourselves in a situation where the Spirit is working and moving, but the expression of this is beyond our comfort zone or understanding, let us not be so quick to reject this as the Spirit's activity based on our own prejudices or preferences. The Spirit may well be working powerfully in someone's life and this person may be reacting to this; in any other situation this would seem like natural cause and effect. Search the Scriptures, seek the Lord, pray for the person to encounter the living God and be changed in the process. Equally, we must recognise that different people connect with God in different ways, and we should structure our meetings to reflect this. Many people meet God by singing their hearts out in the midst of the assembly[579], others find God in the still small voice after the storm.[580] Both of these expressions require sensitivity and need to be nurtured in order to nurture the person's walk with God.

**Four: The Spirit is a person.** While we may not be familiar with the notion of a person being anything other than a human, we could get around this unfamiliarity by simply expanding our definition of what makes someone a 'person'. If we use, as a working hypothesis, the phrase 'a person is anything with a personality' then it may become easier to understand the personhood of the Spirit. Ultimately, we must take it on faith that the Spirit falls into this category, but given that this faith is based on how Jesus refers to

---

[579] Psalm 22:22
[580] 1 Kings 19:12-13

the Spirit, we can happily follow His example. When Jesus speaks of the Spirit, it is always using the personal pronoun 'He'. The Spirit is never referred to as 'it', which would convey ideas of Him being a force or entity, but always as 'He' which denotes a person. Before the incarnation, Jesus (the second person of the Trinity) was of a more similar substance with the Spirit than after the incarnation. John tells us that "The Word became flesh and dwelt among us"[581], implying that Christ wasn't a man in eternity past (but will be for eternity future[582]), but that he became human at a fixed point in time. The Spirit is without a body, and yet dwells within us, He is without a face and yet shows us the face of Christ, and He is without a birthday and yet brings about new birth. **Application:** Once we appreciate and understand that the Spirit is a person to be communicated with and loved as opposed to a force to be wielded or commanded, the manner in which we approach Him can only alter. We can, and should, speak to, pray to and worship the Spirit as readily and freely as we do Jesus or the Father. Understanding the personhood of the Spirit is vital to our relating to the Trinity, with whom we'll be with forevermore.

**Five: Wait for the Lord before doing anything.** As we saw in chapter 12 from both Old and New Testament examples, waiting for the anointing, leading and presence of the Lord before doing any Christian work is essential. It is essential for two reasons; firstly, it affirms the worth we ascribe to the direction of the Spirit, and conveys our high opinion of Him, and secondly, it prevents us from getting carried away with our own ideas. Our ideas may well be good and right and fruitful, but if we are not partnering with the Lord then we are setting ourselves up for difficulties. **Application:** Practice being patient, asking the Spirit to bring about this fruit in our hearts. Weigh any prophetic insight against Scripture, trusted friends and your own conscience. Recognise the potential difficulties of an activity and bring them back to the Lord. Analyse your own heart,

---

[581] John 1:14
[582] Revelation 1:13,17,18

scanning for any unrighteous desire for success or prominence or fame. If, after some honest scrutiny you believe that the Lord is with you, go for it!

**Six: Seeking God should be an on-going action**, not just something done at the start of an activity. There will be many in the Christian world who, when beginning an outreach activity or some other ministry will seek the Lord for guidance. But, when this ministry has gotten off the ground, the focus can shift from seeking the Lord to keeping up the momentum. The problem with this approach is two-fold. Firstly, it implies that we need the help of the Lord God Almighty to get a project going and to manage it when it is small, but once it gets bigger we need less of His help. This is nonsensical. If we need God to help get something going, why would we need less of His help when it *is* going? Secondly, it means that if we are faced with success (which can be more difficult to handle than failure) then we may perpetuate this ministry for reasons other than because it is what God wants us to do; if we are not seeking Him about it honestly, we won't know His thoughts and perspectives on it. We may keep it going for our own personal gain or fame, because it turns a profit, because it is successful and people enjoy it or even 'because this is what we've always done', which is most damaging reason of all. **Application:** Regularly seek God about anything we are doing for Him. Involve the Spirit in all decisions being made, not just at the start of a project but throughout it. This will mean that, even if something closes because it is no longer viable or if it closes when it is at the height of its success, we are dancing to the tune of One, and that's the main thing.

**Seven: Where the Spirit is, God's presence is.** Given that the Spirit dwells within every believer, and that, as we see in numerous Old Testament examples (see chapter 6) as well as in Revelation, being 'in the Spirit' often ushers people into the presence of God, we can safely conclude that the Spirit brings people into God's presence. Too often we can fall into an old covenant mind-set, whereby we find ourselves acting, if not professing, that being 'at church' is where we can meet with God, but in going about our regular lives we cannot. This was true in the old covenant, as the tabernacle or temple was where the presence of God dwelt. But, under the new covenant, the curtain has been torn, the Spirit has been poured into the hearts of believers and the presence of God is where His people are. **Application:** A friend of mine once put it this way during a sermon; "When you're in the pub, God is in the pub." What he meant by this was that we can experience, communicate with, rely on and spend time with God wherever we are, because His Spirit now dwells inside of us. The result of this is that our relationship with God by His Spirit should be galvanised, and we can believe and rely on the fact that we are never alone regardless of our location.

**Eight: There is no place for a clergy/laity divide.** It follows that if the Spirit was given to specific believers and not to others, like we find to be the case in the Old Testament, then it is right and proper to have a divide between the people who have direct access to God (priests, prophets, kings etc.) and those who don't (everyone else). It becomes the job of the priests to commune with God and to pass on His commands and requirements and affections to the people who don't have access to Him themselves. This was the model employed by those in power in the lead up to the Reformation. Whether this was an intentional ploy, a misunderstanding of Scripture or an unfortunate progression of politics is up for debate, and what was the case for one pope or emperor may not be the case for the next. However, it was against this that Martin Luther protested; this was one of the reasons why he translated the Bible into German. Because Latin was the language of the educated and elite at the time, but was entirely inaccessible by the common man, this meant that he had to take as absolute what he was told by the clergy. This should never have happened. Given that the Spirit now (by which I mean since Pentecost) dwells in all believers, all believers now have unlimited access to the Lord, and there is no need to go through any earthly intermediary because Christ is that intermediary. **Application:** I am not advocating a free-for all with no leadership, as leadership within the church is a God-appointed office. What I am saying is that those leaders have a responsibility to encourage the congregation to seek and hear God for themselves, not to tell the people what God would say to them. Leadership is to lead, not to seek to rise above people or control them. Good leadership should recognise that their congregation can read the Bible, pray, worship, hear from God and follow His voice for themselves; the purpose of leadership is to bring people into who God has made them to be.

**Nine: Being Spirit-filled is a normal part of the Christian life.** There is a myth that being filled with the Spirit is either something that happens to only a certain number of people, or that it is something that happens on one occasion and is not repeated. This second part of the myth might go as far as to say that a person is 'filled with the Spirit' automatically when they become a Christian. While this may absolutely be the case for some people, this will very definitely not be the case for others. As we saw in chapter 10, there are multiple occasions in the New Testament where someone's conversion and their experience of being filled with the Spirit happen at two distinct points in time. However, we see no examples of the first churches or their leaders informing and instructing that being filled with the Spirit is unimportant. **Application:** In light of this, if we are to be Bible-believing Christians, we must take it as an imperative to be filled with the Spirit and to see this not as unusual or as a singular event, but as a regular part of our walk with Christ. What this actually looks like will differ from person to person, but what we cannot do is to say that it is unimportant, because Jesus and His first churches certainly didn't see it that way.

**Ten: Being Spirit-filled is necessary for Christian work.** By 'Christian work', I do not mean to limit the scope of being filled with the Spirit to those who are employed by a church or Christian charity or institution. Rather, I mean that Christians will need to be filled with the Spirit in order to be effective Christians in their lives and workplaces, whatever they may be. This is because of the example of the disciples between the resurrection and Pentecost. These few dozen people had seen Jesus murdered and risen from the dead, had a six-week Bible study with Him[583] and seen Him ascend into heaven. But, Jesus effectively says in Luke 24 that there is something that they still lack; "wait until you are clothed with power from on high"[584]. **Application:** Pray to be continually filled with God's Holy Spirit. Have friends pray for you. Some believers, if they are feeling particularly vulnerable or under attack, might 'pray on' the whole armour of God from Ephesians 6. Either way, we have seen from Scripture that being Spirit-filled was a precursor to effective Christian ministry. This we should seek.

**Eleven: We must spend time with the Spirit.** Because the Spirit is a person, albeit one without a physical body, this means that we can spend time with Him. Actually, it means that, if we worship a Trinitarian Christian God, then we *must* spend time with Him. I don't believe that the Spirit is likely to be petty if we choose not to spend time with Him, but equally I believe that if we are to grow into being people who are filled with the Spirit and are seeking to grow in the fruit of the Spirit, actually spending time with Him is essential. **Application:** Make time to pray to and listen to the Spirit. There is ample Biblical basis for the Spirit speaking to people or prompting people to do something; we should not expect His activity today to be any different.

**Twelve: The Spirit is fully God.** Ultimately, the reason why we should listen to anything concerning the Spirit, aside from the Bible's insistence that we do so, is that He is fully God. He is as divine as Jesus or the Father, and to think any less of Him, say, as the third-rung of a deity ladder, is to do Him a disservice. Outlined in chapter 9 is the Biblical basis for the divinity of the Spirit, and we must approach Him as the fully divine person of the Spirit that He is. **Application:** We can pray to Him. We can ask Him for miracles. We can expect Him to understand us and to know us intimately. We can

---

[583] Luke 24:54
[584] Luke 24:49

expect Him to surprise and challenge us, and we can build all of these into our prayer lives.

**Thirteen: 'Unusual' does not necessarily equal 'wrong'.** Charles Wesley once said that he would rather have the illegitimate expressions of the Holy Spirit in amongst the legitimate ones, rather than quash it all and lose both the pure and the counterfeit[585]. There are some churches today which operate by a similar line of reasoning; "Let everything have an airing, the good stuff will dispel the rest." While there is some merit to this perspective, it does have several flaws. Firstly, it reduces the activity of the Holy Spirit to merely external phenomena while ignoring what is happening between Christ and the person's soul. Secondly, it could be opening the door to some unhelpful spiritual activity, but thirdly, it assumes that we have no basis by which to say that X is helpful and godly but Y is unhelpful and of a different origin. I would strongly contest this final point; indeed, this book is an attempt towards establishing firmly who the Holy Spirit is and what His work looks like. Having said that, we can be tempted to go too far the other way and say that anything that is unusual is not of the Holy Spirit, and as such must be resisted and quelled. On many occasions in Scripture do we find evidence of the Holy Spirit doing or creating some very, to our eyes, unusual things. It is beyond our remit to say that we do not like or will not permit something on the *sole* basis that is it unusual.
**Application:** Our churches need to reflect Scripture. If we stop spiritual activity because we find it uncomfortable, or because it doesn't fit our predispositions about what should happen in church or what Christians should value, then we may find ourselves guilty of quenching the Spirit, something we are impelled not to do[586]. Equally, if we take the perspective that 'anything goes' and that anything that anyone believes to be 'by the Holy Spirit' is truly so, then we are breaking the third commandment to not take the Lord's

---

[585] A. Taves, *'Fits, Trances and Visions'*, Princeton: Princeton University Press, 1999, P56 - 58
[586] 1 Thessalonians 5:19-21

name in vain[587]. We reduce and cheapen the ministry of the Spirit by saying, effectively, 'weird = Holy Spirit'. Sometimes weird just equals weird, and has no spiritual merit or scriptural basis. To avoid straying from either side of the path, we should seek the Spirit as we see Him in Scripture.

**Fourteen: The Spirit is personal.** With so much discussion about a theology of the Spirit, it would be easy to overlook the fact that He is not so much something to be discussed, but a personal companion. Jesus said as much in John 14, when He describes the Spirit as 'the helper' or, as the King James Version puts it, 'the comforter'[588]. The Spirit is intimately involved in our prayers, our worries and our triumphs. We can stray too far into a 'theology of the Spirit for the church' without giving much thought to a 'theology of the Spirit for me'. **Application:** We must involve the Spirit in our personal lives. Given that He is fully God, He knows it all anyway, but if we actively involve Him, we treat Him like a person as opposed to a report. A report about you might know every single detail of your life, but a person is involved in a give-and-take relationship whereby details are shared not as the trading of information, but as the joining of hearts. The Spirit is a person who can be grieved or outraged, just as I am a person who can be grieved and outraged; this is a good basis for building a friendship.

**Fifteen: The Spirit brings adoption.** One of the more practical remits of the Holy Spirit is that He is in the business of making former slaves of sin into current and future sons and daughters of God. Paul in Romans describes the Spirit as 'the Spirit of adoption'. This is the process which gloriously completes the human story; created as children of God[589], the relationship is spoiled by sin and we became slaves to it[590], Christ suffered and died to bring many sons to glory[591] and we receive the Spirit of adoption, by which we

---

[587] Exodus 20:7, see page 167 for an expansion of this point.
[588] John 14:16
[589] Luke 3:38
[590] John 8:34

cry Abba Father[592]! Scripture repeatedly affirms that we are adopted sons and daughters of God by the Spirit[593]. **Application:** If we truly embrace that we have been brought into the fellowship and love of the King of the universe, that through Christ He sees us as His children and not as filthy sinners, that while we were formally sinners, we are presently and will be forevermore sons of God, and that future glory overwhelms our past failures, how can we fail to cry out in worship to our Abba Father?

**Sixteen: The Spirit leads people to God.** The first chapter of Genesis describes the Spirit as "hovering over the face of the waters" in a world that was formless and void[594]. This can be seen as a metaphor for how the Spirit works on people's hearts before they even know it. The Spirit leads people to God, sometimes through trial, sometimes through 'mountain-top moments', but if it is the Spirit working, He is leading people closer to their heavenly Father. This applies to people who want nothing to do with God and to people who have been Christians for decades; there is always more. Of course, God gave humanity free will, and we are not and never forced to do or be anything against our will, but just like the expert chess player will position his pieces in such a way to force the person they are playing with to make certain moves, the Spirit is always at work and always pointing us towards Christ. **Application:** As Paul concludes his letter to the Ephesians, we should pray "at all times in the Spirit, with all prayer and supplication... making supplication for all the saints"[595]. There is an element of trust in this matter; for that loved one, friend, neighbour, colleague or celebrity we must pray for them and trust that the Spirit will work on them to lead them to Jesus.

---

[591] Hebrews 2:10
[592] Romans 8:15
[593] See chapter 4
[594] Genesis 1:2
[595] Ephesians 6:18

**Seventeen: The Spirit's 'method' of conversion varies from situation to situation.** In addition to trusting the Spirit with a loved one, we must recognise that different people come to Christ in different ways. The Spirit does not use a one-size-fits-all technique, presumably because people are not all one size. Some people experience a 'bolt of lightning' moment, whereby they are arrested by the risen Christ and immediately converted[596]. Others are brought to Christ after hearing a sermon, when all the pieces drop into place at the right moment and they give their lives to Him[597]. Still others witness a miracle and conclude that there must be a God[598], and others are flooded with the Holy Spirit and just know in a way that surpasses knowledge (to paraphrase Paul in Ephesians 3:19) that Jesus is Lord. **Application:** Let us not be prescriptive concerning issues about which the Bible is not prescriptive. We can all too readily succumb to the temptation of thinking that the way we were converted, or the most frequent way you see someone be converted, is the 'correct' way. This is not the case. The Spirit moves differently with different people, and what we may find attempting to stay 'correct' is that we exclude this or that method because it is unfamiliar to us. Let us let the Spirit decide how to win souls for Jesus; He's been doing it a lot longer than we have.

**Eighteen: The Spirit builds up.** While it is entirely feasible to be assured of our place in heaven as a 'lone ranger Christian', being brought into our full purpose in God's eternal plan is not possible without being part of a church. Paul's description of the church as the body of Christ in 1 Corinthians 12 makes a very keen point; an ear, and eye or a hand will die if separated from the rest of the body. On the other hand, being connected to the body will cause these parts to thrive and be at their most useful and fulfilled. In a similar way, if we are to fully realise all that God has for us in Christ, we need to fellowship with other believers. One of the reasons for

---

[596] Acts 9:3-19
[597] Acts 2:14-41
[598] Hebrews 2:4

this is that the Spirit builds up the church, and as such we need to be connected to this God-given family (never intended to be a stuffy institution) if we are to benefit and be built up. This is because the Spiritual gifts are given to build up the church[599], and Christ gives gifts to the church[600]. **Application:** The Spirit is in the business of building up the church. We should react in two ways to this; Firstly, let us emulate the Spirit in building people up. This does not mean being blind to their imperfections, but rather showing grace as we have been shown grace. Grace specifically means receiving goodness without meriting it. Let us therefore be graceful and loving and hopeful and kind towards people, praising them for their efforts in public, but bringing any correction in the same spirit in private. Secondly, we should recognise that while the church is led by people with failures and shortcomings, she is Christ's church being built by God's people in partnership with God's Spirit. We should be careful of how we speak of the church. Should we be as James writes in his epistle?

> "With [our tongues] we bless our Lord and Father, and with it we curse people who are made in the likeness of God"[601].

God forbid.

**Nineteen: The Spirit inspires for a reason.** This is a somewhat self-contained point, but when the Spirit inspires someone to do something, that inspiration should have a tangible outcome. This might not mean an outwardly visible outcome, as the Spirit might be inspiring us to think a different way rather than act in a different way, but the result should be a change somewhere in our lives. **Application:** We must firstly learn to discern the Spirit's voice as distinct from our own thoughts or those of someone else. This might be a 'turning in our Spirit', it might be that itch in our conscience, it might be that Scripture which won't leave you alone; we must

---

[599] 1 Corinthians 14:12
[600] Ephesians 4:11
[601] James 3:9

determine how the Spirit speaks to us. Secondly, we must practise acting on His promptings. This is stepping out in faith. The deed of acting upon the prompting of the Spirit is a faith-building exercise, regardless of the result. If the Spirit is a person and is fully God, He can be trusted and we can have faith in Him.

**Twenty: The Spirit still inspires today.** If this statement is not true, then we have truly wasted our time; I in writing this book and you in reading it. While someone holding a cessationist view might find the proceeding dozen chapters interesting, without being convinced of their accuracy, these arguments are not of any worth for their Christian walk. This is one of the core reasons why I believe in the on-going work of the Holy Spirit; it means I don't have to do it by myself. I have been given the Spirit of God to live inside me, to reveal the love of God to me, to guide and instruct me, to be my comforter and my friend. With no substantiated break between the New Testament era and the contemporary church, we are compelled to conclude that the Spirit still inspires us today. **Application:** We must expect this. We must organise our lives and our churches around the fact that the Spirit is living and active and will be speaking to us about our lives and churches. We must act when we hear Him, listen when we don't and believe in both instances.

### Final Thoughts

My intention in writing this book has been to establish a firm ground for believing in the continuing work of the Holy Spirit. What we have seen from some 300 verses is that sometimes the Spirit appears to be 'weird' to our eyes, and sometimes He is entirely 'not weird'. What I would say is this; if someone claims that such-and-such an expression is happening 'by the Holy Spirit', but no Biblical examples or precedent can be found, this expression should be rejected as counterfeit. Equally, we must be continually searching the Scriptures to be refreshing our theology, as the 'Bible in our heads' is often somewhat different from the Bible on the page.

Finally, I firmly believe that we need to humbly return to Scripture as our daily bread to invigorate and empower our theology. The title of this book is 'Incessant Theology', which is both a pun on the word 'cessationist' and a smiling nod to William Rees. However, there is a more fundamental philosophy behind this title. While Christ is the final revelation, and the Bible is the completed Word of God to us, our understanding should never stop being informed, updated and revitalised. Because we worship a living Person, because the Spirit of the infinite God lives within finite me and you, we cannot afford to stop seeking and searching. We will not, on this side of eternity, get to a point where we 'know everything' nor have all of our theology irrevocably nailed down. We must always return to Scripture and search it with the help of the Spirit to enable us to see new elements which, in previous readings, we may have ignored, been blind to or overlooked. Our theology should be a work in progress. All theology should, at its core, be incessant theology.

# Fourteen

# Epilogue

## ✳✳✳

I do not believe I am wrong about anything in this book; if I did I would have changed what I thought was wrong to be what I believed was right. However, I didn't think I was wrong about my perspective of the Holy Spirit a year or 5 years ago. To that end, in the spirit of theology being incessant, should you have any questions, comments or requests concerning anything contained in these pages, please get in touch using one of the following methods:

Website:            www.IncessantTheology.com

Email:              info@IncessantTheology.com

Facebook:           www.facebook.com/IncessantTheology

Twitter:            www.twitter.com/IncessantTHLGY

# Fifteen

# Appendix 1 - Research

## ✳✳✳

In chapter 10, I mentioned some research I had conducted concerning the correlation between conversion and the expression of the supernatural gifts of the Holy Spirit. What follows is a summary of this research, which was conducted in 2008 and 2009 and pertains to the city of Glasgow. While I believe that Glasgow was not an exceptional case, it would go beyond the scope of the research to extrapolate a trend that could be applicable to any other area. If you would like to see the full and completed work, please email info@IncessantTheology.com with the phrase 'Holy Spirit Conversion Research' in the subject line.

The research was an analysis of the statement; "Churches who demonstrate the supernatural gifts of the Holy Spirit on a weekly basis will see more people become Christians than churches which never have any such demonstrations."

My research showed that the frequency with which the gifts of the Holy Spirit are demonstrated within a church *does* have an effect on the number of conversions that church will see. More specifically, it appears that in 2008, a church which saw (at least) weekly demonstrations of the supernatural gifts of the Holy Spirit saw an average of 6.8 conversions, while each church that never saw any such demonstrations saw an average of 2.2 conversions during the same period of time.

This indication that more people become Christians in 'weekly' frequency churches is supported by the results for the total number of conversions between 1984 and 2009; an average of 5.9 people becoming Christians per church, per year in 'weekly' frequency churches over this time period. A comparison of this with 'never' frequency churches yields a thought provoking result; in such churches, an average of 2 people became Christians per church, per year between 1984 and 2009.

In conclusion, it seems clear that there is much to be said for the claim that churches who demonstrate the supernatural gifts of the Holy Spirit on a weekly basis will see more people become Christians than churches which never have any such demonstrations; somewhere in the region of three times as many. While this is not the only way in which a person will become convinced that Jesus is the Christ, and indeed, exposure to the Bible would certainly be a sizable contender, exposure to miraculous occurrences can, in some cases, produce a sense of awe and wonder that leads to conversion, as this research suggests.

# Sixteen

# Glossary

### ✳✳✳

1.  Exegesis (or Exegetical)
    *   The process of taking out from a text what the authors, both human and divine, originally intended to be understood by it. The purpose of this is to seek an accurate interpretation of what the passage in question said to its original readers as well as to us today.

2.  Eisegesis (or Eisegetical)
    *   The opposite of exegesis. To read the Bible eisegetically is to read *into* the text something which it doesn't necessarily say. Eisegesis is easy to slip into, because it is impossible to be entirely unbiased when reading the Bible, but it must be avoided at all costs if we are to honestly take from Scripture what God put in it. Eisegesis is to use Scripture to justify our own position; exegesis is to investigate what God says about a topic.

3.  Cessationist
    *   A Christian who believes that, upon the completion of the Bible and the death of the last of the twelve apostles in about 100 A.D., the supernatural activity of the Holy Spirit ceased. This is most often used in relation to supernatural gifts of the Spirit.

4.  Continuationist
    *   A Christian who believes that the Holy Spirit continues to operate today in the same manner which we see in the New Testament. A continuationist believes that the

supernatural activity of the Holy Spirit can be experienced in churches today.

5. Protestants
- Protestants are, literally, 'those who protest'. In this context, I refer to Protestants as distinct from Roman Catholic or Orthodox Christians who, to some degree, follow the teachings of the reformers Martin Luther, John Calvin and Ulrich Zwingli, among others. Protestants believe that the Bible, and not the established church or the Pope, is the highest authority given to humanity by God.

6. Reformed (or Calvinist)
- A Christian who is reformed believes in the principles of exegetical study of the Bible, as they believe it is the highest authority given to humanity by God. John Calvin, one of the first reformers, is generally seen as being the father of the reformed faith. Reformed Christians prize the centrality of prayer and preaching, as well as having a very high view of the sovereignty of God.

7. Evangelicals
- Evangelicals are a loose association of believers and churches who have a passion for spreading the Gospel of Jesus Christ. Evangelicals believe that Jesus literally died and rose again, and that His doing so he took away our sins. Evangelicals also believe that everyone needs to 'be saved' from their sins in order to A) understand all that God intended them to be and B) avoid the perils of Hell. Finally, evangelicals also believe that the Bible is the ultimate authority and governs the way they live their lives and act in the world.

8. Atonement (or atoning sacrifice, or 'work of Christ on the cross')

   • The atonement is the term given to what Jesus' death accomplished. Rather than being seen as a horrible accident, it is viewed as the intention of Christ being sent to earth by the Father. The atonement refers to the death of Jesus making the way for the re-establishing of a relationship between sinful people and a Holy God. There are a variety of views about the nature of the atonement (i.e. exactly what happened to reconnect God and His people), but almost all of these are agreed that when Jesus died, He died in our place, and as a result I can be forgiven of my sins and enter a relationship with God.

9. Over-realised eschatology

   • Over-realised eschatology is a branch of theology which goes beyond what conventional Christian doctrine would say about the extent of Christ's victory on the cross. Someone with an over-realised eschatology might believe that certain benefits of Christ's victory are available to the church in the present day, whereas others would argue that such benefits are only available in the new heavens and the new earth and are not for the present day. An example of this concerns physical healing; pain and death came into the world through Adam but Christ died on the cross in our place, thereby undoing the curse which God placed on the earth in Genesis 3. An over-realised eschatology would claim that when Jesus said "it is finished", then all of the bad effects of Adam's sin were undone, including sickness, and this *should* be realised in the present day. A problem with this claim is it blurs the line between the 'now' and the 'not yet', and ignores the fact that the Bible speaks of salvation, redemption and healing in the past, present and future tenses. It is my hope to explore and discuss this topic in greater depth in a future book.

10. Pentecost
- The outpouring of the Spirit upon the church in Jerusalem after the ascension of Jesus, as prophesied about in Joel 2 and fulfilled in Acts 2.

11. Omniscient
- The theological term for 'all knowing'. This is an attribute of God's which means that all knowledge, past, present and future are accessible to Him at any given moment in time. As such He "knows the end from the beginning"[602].

---

[602] Isaiah 46:10

# Seventeen

# Bibliography

## ∗∗∗

Books referenced

1.  F.F. Bruce (ed), *New International Bible Commentary*, Michigan: Zondervan, 1979, p120

2.  C. Duriez, *Tolkien and C.S. Lewis: The Gift of Friendship*, USA: Paulist Press, 2003, p80

3.  W. Grudem, Systematic Theology, Nottingham: Inter Varsity Press, 2007, p233

4.  Brother Yun and P. Hattaway, *The Heavenly Man*, Oxford: Monarch Books, 2009, pp38-39

5.  M. Luther, '*The Babylonian Captivity of the Church*', Philadelphia Edition, 1520, Volume 2, p241

6.  D. K. McKim, *The Cambridge Companion to Martin Luther*, Cambridge: Cambridge Univeristy Press, 2003, p145

7.  A. Plass, '*The Theatrical Tapes of Leonard Thynn*', London: Marshall Pickering, 1989, p1

8.  M. Sandel, *Justice*, London: Penguin, 2010, p108

9.  J. R. W. Stott, *The Preacher's Portrait*, Michigan: Eerdmans Publishing, 1961, page 118

10. A. Taves, *Fits, Trances and Visions*, Princeton: Princeton University Press, 1999, P56 – 58

11. T. Virgo, '*The Spirit-Filled Church*', Oxford: Monarch Books, 2011, p47

12. R. Warren, *The Purpose Driven Church*, Michigan: Zondervan, 1995, p77

Online sources referenced

13. http://www.scripture4all.org/OnlineInterlinear/NTpdf/joh16.pdf, retrieved 2/4/2014

14. http://www.blueletterbible.org/lang/lexicon/lexicon.cfm?Strongs =G1515andt=KJV, retrieved 8/2/2013

15. Nicky Gumble, https://twitter.com/nickygumbel/status/299640361746309120, retrieved 8/2/2013

16. Rick Warren, Facebook 9th November 2013, https://www.facebook.com/pastorrickwarren/posts/1015203627 9630903, retrieved 9/4/2014

Other media referenced

17. 'Finding Nemo', 2003. Film. Directed by Andrew Stanton. USA: Buena Vista Pictures

18. U2, "Original of the Species", How to Dismantle an Atomic Bomb, Island Records, 2004

19. Spiderman, 2002. Film. Directed by Sam RAIMI. USA: Columbia Pictures

"In Thy truth Thou dost direct me
By Thy Spirit through Thy Word;
And Thy grace my need is meeting,
As I trust in Thee, my Lord.


Of Thy fullness Thou art pouring
Thy great love and pow'r on me,
Without measure, full and boundless,
Drawing out my heart to Thee."


'Here is Love'

William Rees, 1900

# About the author

Alan P Harrison was born in the north-east of England, where he lived until he was 18. After spending 5 months in India with Scripture Union following the Boxing Day Tsunami, he returned to the UK and moved to Glasgow to study Theology at the International Christian College. After 4 years of study, he graduated with an honours degree in Theology, specialising in the practical application of theology to Christian life.

He later gained a PGDE in secondary-level Religious Education, and currently teaches Religious, Moral and Philosophical studies in a secondary school in the west of Scotland.

Alan is married to his high-school-sweetheart, Sarah, and they have a son, Desmond. They are members of Hope Church Glasgow, which is part of the NewFrontiers family of churches.